Life Through Angel Eyes

CH Jodi M Dehn

Published by Tamerlane Media, 2025.

While every precaution has been taken in the preparation of this book, the publisher assumes no responsibility for errors or omissions, or for damages resulting from the use of the information contained herein.

LIFE THROUGH ANGEL EYES

First edition. February 9, 2025.

Copyright © 2025 CH Jodi M Dehn.

ISBN: 979-8989852451

Written by CH Jodi M Dehn.

REVIEWS

"Are you ready to learn a new way to deal with anxiety, grief, forgiveness, purpose? We all need this from time to time, don't you think? Chaplain Jodi has done just that with her connections to the angelic realm and beyond. This book will help you see how you can let go and allow the angels to show you the way. Open your heart, and, as Jodi always says 'activate those angels'!"

Sarah Lemos-Aune, internationally known psychic medium and television celebrity

"Life Through Angel Eyes is an insightful and comprehensive book that delves into the world of archangels, and how they can be called upon for guidance. The author does a fantastic job of making the subject accessible to both newcomers and those already familiar with angelic lore. This book is well-researched and thoughtfully organized, making it a valuable resource for anyone interested in spiritual growth and angelic assistance. Whether you're seeking comfort, guidance, or a deeper understanding of the spiritual realm, this resource guide offers a wealth of knowledge and inspiration."

Ken Boggle, psychic medium and star of Living for the Dead

INTRODUCTION

There are whispers in the unseen, soft voices carried on a divine current—reminders, guidance, messages that brush against our hearts when we least expect them. Angels are not distant; they walk with us, soul protectors tethered to the light of the Divine. They are guardians, yes, but also messengers of truths we sometimes cannot see: paths we must follow, lessons we must learn, and barriers we must release.

When life pulls us away from our soul's purpose—when doubt lingers, the heart wavers, or our spirit feels heavy—it is the angels who nudge us back to clarity. Their messages are not loud proclamations, but quiet invitations to shift, to notice, to remember who we truly are. They offer a lantern in the dark, a hand when we stumble, and words that breathe life into the parts of us we thought had faded.

This book is a sacred gathering of those messages—a collection of angelic insights tailored to the most human of experiences. Here you will find the voices of 14 archangels, each with their own wisdom to share, yet all connected in their mission: to bring you home to yourself. From navigating relationships and healing grief to finding balance, forgiveness, and purpose, their words will act as mirrors and maps, reflecting back what your soul most needs and showing you how to move forward.

Archangel Michael, the shield and protector, will remind you of your strength when fear tries to take root. Gabriel, the angel of communication and joy, will teach you to speak your truth and find your voice. Raphael will gently guide you toward healing—physical, emotional, and spiritual—while Uriel will illuminate wisdom in the darkest of times. Each angel, fourteen is this book, steps forward with purpose, offering a unique key to unlock the next door on your journey.

Here, you will discover truths about the heart's resilience, the mind's power to shift, and the soul's longing for alignment. The angels will help you untangle confusion, face struggles with grace, and embrace the beauty of being alive in both the joyful and difficult moments. They will hold space for your questions and reveal answers not as quick fixes, but as timeless wisdom meant to nourish your spirit.

This is more than a book—it's a resource book, it is a conversation with the Divine through the voices of those sent to guide you. As you read, you are invited to listen—not just with your ears, but with your heart, your intuition, and the knowing deep within. You will not be alone as you explore these words. The angels are already here, walking beside you, whispering encouragement and waiting to be called upon.

Within these pages reside their light, their love, and their guidance. Call on them in light and love. Then simply open your heart, quiet your mind, and allow yourself to receive. The angels are speaking. Are you ready to listen?

Activate Your Angels

ON ANXIETY

Archangel Michael

On Anxiety:

Anxiety is a shadow that thrives on uncertainty and fear. I stand ready to shield you from negativity and remind you of your inner strength. When doubts creep in, I can cut through them with clarity. Call on me to establish boundaries, protect your peace, and release unnecessary burdens. Remember, courage is not the absence of fear but the mastery of it.

Talk to me:

"Archangel Michael, I call upon you to shield me from fear and doubts that fuel my anxiety. Help me release what no longer serves me and create boundaries for a peaceful mind. Thank you for your unwavering strength and protection."

Archangel Gabriel

On Anxiety:

Anxiety silences your voice, leaving you unable to connect or express your true self. I bring clarity and inspiration, replacing guilt with self-acceptance. Let me help you rediscover joy in your heart and unlock your creativity. Together, we'll transform hesitations into confidence, allowing your authentic self to shine.

Talk to me:

"Archangel Gabriel, I ask for your guidance in overcoming the fears that block my voice. Help me find clarity, joy, and confidence in expressing myself. Thank you for reigniting my creativity and connection to others."

Archangel Raphael

On Anxiety:

Anxiety takes a toll on both your mind and body, creating tension and imbalance. I offer a soothing presence to calm your spirit and release physical strain. With every breath, I bring healing energy to cleanse your worries. Let me help you uncover the hidden lessons and gifts within your challenges so they no longer weigh you down.

Talk to me:

"Archangel Raphael, please soothe my mind and heal the physical toll anxiety has taken on me. Help me breathe deeply, release tension, and find the hidden blessings in my struggles. Thank you for your healing light."

Archangel Uriel

On Anxiety:

When fear overwhelms you, it clouds your judgment and blocks peace. I bring the wisdom to help you see clearly through the storm. Anxiety often feels like chaos, but within it lies the seed of growth. Let me help you find the calm within and discover the ideas and perspectives that will guide you to peace.

Talk to me:

"Archangel Uriel, grant me wisdom to understand my fears and guide me toward calm clarity. Help me transform anxiety into opportunities for growth and renewal. Thank you for your enlightening presence."

LIFE THROUGH ANGEL EYES

Archangel Zadkiel

On Anxiety:

Anxiety can trap you in a cycle of self-criticism and regret. I am here to help you release the weight of unprocessed emotions and find forgiveness—for yourself and others. Together, we will bring comfort to your heart, calm your racing thoughts, and create space for discernment and wisdom to flourish.

Talk to me;

"Archangel Zadkiel, I ask for your help in releasing past regrets and finding forgiveness within myself. Please bring calm and clarity to my thoughts, replacing anxiety with comfort and wisdom. Thank you for your compassionate guidance."

Archangel Chamuel

On Anxiety:

Anxiety can make you feel disconnected from love and peace, leaving you with a sense of emptiness. I bring healing to the wounds of abandonment and emotional pain, guiding you toward self-love and inner harmony. Let me help you nurture your inner child and replace impulsive fears with a deep sense of calm.

Talk to me:

"Archangel Chamuel, help me heal the wounds that feed my anxiety and reconnect with self-love. Guide me toward inner peace and help me nurture the parts of me that feel lost. Thank you for your loving support."

Archangel Jophiel

On Anxiety:

Anxiety dims your perspective, making everything seem heavier than it truly is. I am here to shine a light on the beauty that surrounds you and to shift your thoughts toward gratitude and possibility. Together, we can transform negative thought patterns into ones that help you manifest your highest goals and live in understanding.

Talk to me:

"Archangel Jophiel, please help me see the beauty and gratitude in my life, even in challenging moments. Transform my anxious thoughts into ones of clarity and understanding. Thank you for your illuminating presence."

Archangel Laviah

On Anxiety:

Anxiety often rises when you feel disconnected from your intuition. I bring revelations through dreams and deep inner knowing. Let me help you explore the messages hidden within, so you can find clarity and trust in your path. Your intuition is a powerful guide, and I am here to strengthen it.

Talk to me:

"Archangel Laviah, I ask for your guidance through dreams and intuition to uncover the truths I need to find peace. Please help me reconnect to my inner wisdom. Thank you for your enlightening guidance."

Archangel Sandalphon

On Anxiety:

LIFE THROUGH ANGEL EYES

When anxiety becomes overwhelming, it's a sign that you've lost your grounding. I help you reconnect to the Earth's steady rhythm and find harmony. Music and stillness are powerful tools to calm the aggressive energy within. Together, we'll root you in the present, where peace resides.

Talk to me:

"Archangel Sandalphon, please help me find grounding and harmony when anxiety overtakes me. Bring the soothing power of music and stillness into my life. Thank you for your calming energy."

Archangel Jeremiel

On Anxiety:

Anxiety often signals unresolved emotions that need clarity and release. I help you reflect on your feelings with compassion, bringing forgiveness and understanding. Together, we can create a vision for positive change, turning emotional chaos into a foundation for peace and progress.

Talk to me:

"Archangel Jeremiel, I ask for your help in bringing clarity to my emotions and guiding me toward forgiveness. Help me transform anxiety into a plan for positive change. Thank you for your loving wisdom."

Archangel Raguel

On Anxiety:

Anxiety thrives on misunderstandings—both within your relationships and your inner self. I bring harmony to the chaos, helping you discern the truth behind your fears. Let me calm the tension that clouds your mind and realign your heart with peace. Together, we'll restore balance to your thoughts and connections, allowing you to trust yourself and others again. You are not alone in this.

Talk to Me:

"Archangel Raguel, please calm my anxious mind and bring harmony to my thoughts and relationships. Help me overcome misunderstandings and guide me back to peace and balance. Thank you for your loving care."

Archangel Raziel

On Anxiety:

Anxiety can feel like an unknown force pressing down on you, and I am here to illuminate its roots. Often, the wisdom of your soul holds the answers. Let me help you uncover past memories, spiritual insights, or hidden truths that explain and calm your fears. Together, we'll transform confusion into clarity, guiding you to embrace trust in yourself and the divine.

Talk to Me:

"Archangel Raziel, help me uncover the deeper truths and spiritual insights behind my anxiety. Illuminate the wisdom I need to find peace and clarity. Thank you for your guiding light."

Archangel Haniel

On Anxiety:

Anxiety disrupts harmony, creating a storm of worry and restlessness. I bring the energy of balance and grace to restore your inner calm. Let me help you release the frustrations and disappointments that feed your fears. Together, we'll bring your emotions into alignment and renew your sense of peace and trust in life's flow.

Talk to Me:

"Archangel Haniel, please bring harmony to my heart and mind as I navigate anxiety. Help me release fear and restore my emotional balance. Thank you for your calming grace."

ON DEPRESSION

Archangel Michael

On Depression:

Depression can leave you feeling vulnerable, as though the light has faded from your world. I am here to stand by your side, shielding you from the darkness and lifting your spirit with courage. Together, we'll set boundaries to protect your energy and release the fears that weigh you down. You are stronger than this shadow, and I will help you remember your power.

Talk to Me:

"Archangel Michael, I call on you for protection against the shadows of depression. Help me release fear and find the strength to create clear boundaries for my peace. Thank you for your steadfast encouragement and light."

Archangel Gabriel

On Depression:

Depression often stifles your ability to communicate or connect with joy. I bring the energy of renewal, helping you find the courage to express your emotions and rediscover happiness. Together, we will transform guilt into grace and awaken your creative spirit to bring light back into your life.

Talk to Me:

"Archangel Gabriel, please guide me in rediscovering joy and expressing my emotions freely. Help me release guilt and awaken my creativity to bring light into my world. Thank you for your gentle encouragement."

Archangel Raphael

On Depression:

Depression affects your body, mind, and soul, draining your vitality. I bring healing to soothe your heart and physical being, offering peace to your restless mind. Together, we'll uncover the gifts hidden in these dark moments and use them to lead you toward wholeness and light. Healing begins with hope.

Talk to Me:

"Archangel Raphael, please bring healing to my heart, body, and mind as I struggle with depression. Help me see the gifts in my challenges and guide me toward wholeness. Thank you for your compassionate presence."

Archangel Uriel

On Depression:

Despair is a deep weight, but it is not the end of your story. I offer you wisdom to navigate through the darkness and bring peace to your troubled heart. Together, we will uncover new ideas and paths to renewal, turning even the deepest pain into seeds of hope and light.

Talk to Me:

"Archangel Uriel, help me find peace and wisdom in the midst of depression. Guide me toward new perspectives and restore hope in my heart. Thank you for your calming guidance."

CH JODI M DEHN

Archangel Zadkiel

On Depression:

Depression clouds your spirit, weighing you down with heavy emotions. I bring calm and comfort, helping you release self-blame and find forgiveness for yourself and others. Let us clear away the fog of despair and replace it with discernment, strength, and the wisdom to see your worth.

Talk to Me:

"Archangel Zadkiel, I ask for your calm and comfort in my battle with depression. Help me release self-blame, forgive, and find clarity in my thoughts. Thank you for your loving support."

Archangel Metatron

On Depression:

Depression can diminish your self-esteem and make you feel disconnected from your purpose. I am here to help you see your divine light and reconnect with the truth of who you are. Together, we will uncover your unique path to enlightenment and restore the confidence within you.

Talk to Me:

"Archangel Metatron, please guide me to rediscover my self-worth and purpose. Help me embrace my divine light and find clarity in my journey. Thank you for your inspiring wisdom."

Archangel Chamuel

On Depression:

Depression often stems from a lack of self-love and unresolved pain. I bring healing to your heart, nurturing the wounds of abandonment and emotional turmoil. Together, we will replace despair with peace, rekindle love for yourself, and bring harmony to your inner child.

Talk to Me:

"Archangel Chamuel, help me heal the pain that fuels my depression and guide me toward self-love. Bring peace to my heart and nurture the parts of me that feel broken. Thank you for your comforting presence."

Archangel Samuel

On Depression:

Depression can deplete your vitality, leaving you feeling numb and disconnected. I am here to help you restore your energy and heal from past traumas. Together, we'll renew your sense of vitality and bring restful sleep to recharge your spirit.

Talk to Me:

"Archangel Samuel, please restore my energy and help me heal from the traumas that weigh me down. Bring me restful sleep and guide me toward renewal. Thank you for your compassionate strength."

Archangel Zachariel

On Depression:

Depression can lead to self-destructive tendencies and feelings of weakness. I am here to help you uncover your inner strength and face your struggles with courage. Together, we'll navigate the challenges and find solutions to replace destructive habits with empowering choices.

Talk to Me:

"Archangel Zachariel, please guide me in overcoming destructive tendencies and finding strength within myself. Help me face my challenges with courage and clarity. Thank you for your steadfast guidance."

Archangel Jophiel

On Depression:

Depression clouds your perception, making it hard to see the beauty in life. I am here to remind you of the gratitude and light that still exist around you. Together, we'll transform unhealthy thoughts into inspiration, helping you see the beauty in every moment and manifest brighter goals.

Talk to Me:

"Archangel Jophiel, help me shift my thoughts to gratitude and rediscover the beauty in life. Guide me in replacing despair with inspiration and help me manifest brighter possibilities. Thank you for your uplifting light."

Archangel Laviah

On Depression:

Depression can disconnect you from your intuition, leaving you adrift in darkness. I help you explore the messages of your dreams and inner wisdom to reveal clarity and purpose. Let me guide you toward a deeper connection with yourself and your path forward.

Talk to Me:

LIFE THROUGH ANGEL EYES

"Archangel Laviah, please help me explore the wisdom of my dreams and reconnect with my intuition. Guide me toward clarity and purpose. Thank you for your insightful presence."

Archangel Sandalphon

On Depression:

Depression often pulls you out of alignment with the grounding rhythm of life. I bring the steady energy of Earth and the harmony of music to soothe your spirit. Together, we'll replace heaviness with balance and help you find peace in the present moment.

Talk to Me:

"Archangel Sandalphon, please help me find grounding and balance as I navigate depression. Bring harmony and peace into my life through your steady presence. Thank you for your comforting guidance."

Archangel Jeremiel

On Depression:

Depression can trap you in unresolved emotions and hinder your ability to move forward. I am here to help you reflect on your feelings with compassion and plan for positive change. Together, we'll turn emotional chaos into a foundation for healing and hope.

Talk to Me:

"Archangel Jeremiel, guide me in processing my emotions and creating a path toward healing. Help me transform depression into clarity and positive change. Thank you for your loving wisdom."

Archangel Raguel

On Depression:

Depression often fosters misunderstandings, causing disconnection and strain in relationships or within your own heart. I bring the gift of reconciliation, soothing strained emotions and restoring clarity to your perceptions. Let me help you rebuild trust in yourself and others, lifting the weight of isolation and despair. Together, we'll weave understanding and love back into your world.

Talk to Me:

"Archangel Raguel, guide me in mending misunderstandings and restoring harmony to my relationships and my heart. Help me find clarity and trust again. Thank you for your steady presence."

Archangel Raziel

On Depression:

Depression often dims the light of understanding and makes you feel disconnected from your spiritual essence. I offer insights that transcend the limits of time and space—past life memories, divine wisdom, and the understanding that love and light are eternal. Together, we'll lift the veil of sadness and reconnect you to the infinite joy and purpose of your soul.

Talk to Me:

"Archangel Raziel, guide me in uncovering the spiritual truths that bring light to my depression. Help me reconnect with the love and joy that are eternal. Thank you for your enlightening presence."

Archangel Haniel

On Depression:

LIFE THROUGH ANGEL EYES

Depression often arises when the natural rhythms of life feel disrupted, leaving you in a state of imbalance and despair. I offer the gift of harmony to realign your emotions and restore grace to your spirit. Together, we'll gently ease the heaviness in your heart, replacing it with tranquility and hope.

Talk to Me:

"Archangel Haniel, guide me toward balance and grace as I work through my depression. Help me find peace and harmony in my heart again. Thank you for your loving support."

ON GRIEF

Archangel Michael

On Grief:

Grief can leave you feeling defenseless, as though your foundation has crumbled. I am here to shield you from the despair that seeks to overwhelm you. Let me fortify your spirit and remind you of your strength. Together, we'll release the guilt, fear, or self-doubt that often comes with loss. While you mourn, I will protect your heart from being consumed by pain. You are safe to grieve, but know you are never alone.

Talk to Me:

"Archangel Michael, I ask for your protection and strength as I navigate my grief. Help me release fear, guilt, and self-doubt while honoring my feelings. Thank you for standing by me as a steady light."

Archangel Gabriel

On Grief:

Grief silences joy and makes it hard to express the emotions locked within. I am here to help you articulate your pain and reconnect with your heart's voice. Tears are a form of release, and every word spoken in honesty is a step toward healing. Together, we'll move from sorrow into renewal, finding joy and creativity even amidst loss.

Talk to Me:

LIFE THROUGH ANGEL EYES

"Archangel Gabriel, guide me in expressing my grief and finding my voice in the midst of sorrow. Help me reconnect to joy and creativity as I heal. Thank you for your loving support."

Archangel Raphael

On Grief:

Grief touches not just the heart, but the body and soul as well. The weight of loss can make you feel unbalanced and drained. I bring healing to soothe your physical and emotional pain, restoring your energy. Let me help you uncover the gifts hidden within this sorrow—the growth, the love, and the strength that remains. Healing is not forgetting; it is transforming.

Talk to Me:

"Archangel Raphael, please bring healing to my body, mind, and soul as I navigate my grief. Help me find peace and uncover the gifts within my sorrow. Thank you for your comforting presence."

Archangel Uriel

On Grief:

Grief can feel like a storm of despair, leaving you without direction. I bring wisdom to help you see beyond the pain and peace to quiet your heart. While loss is profound, it can also offer insights into life's fragility and beauty. Together, we'll find a way to honor your loved one while bringing tranquility back to your soul.

Talk to Me:

"Archangel Uriel, please guide me with wisdom and bring peace to my heart in this time of grief. Help me honor my loss while finding clarity and strength to move forward. Thank you for your light."

Archangel Zadkiel

On Grief:

Grief often carries unspoken guilt, regret, or unresolved emotions. I am here to help you find forgiveness—for yourself and others—and to bring calm to your heart. Together, we'll transform sorrow into acceptance and clear away the heavy weight of "what-ifs" and "should-haves." Peace begins with compassion, and I am here to remind you of your inner strength.

Talk to Me:

"Archangel Zadkiel, help me release the guilt and regrets that come with grief. Bring calm to my heart and guide me toward forgiveness and acceptance. Thank you for your gentle strength."

Archangel Metatron

On Grief:

Grief can make you question your purpose and self-worth, as though part of you has been lost. I am here to remind you of your divine light and guide you to see the higher purpose within your sorrow. The love you shared is eternal, and through this grief, we can uncover a deeper connection to your soul's journey.

Talk to Me:

"Archangel Metatron, please help me find meaning and purpose within my grief. Remind me of my divine light and guide me to see the higher purpose in my loss. Thank you for your wisdom and love."

Archangel Chamuel

On Grief:

Loss often leaves a void in the heart, awakening feelings of abandonment and self-doubt. I bring love and comfort to that aching space, helping you find peace and reconnect with your inner child. Together, we'll heal the wounds that loss creates and nurture the love that remains. You are not alone, and the love you've shared is forever.

Talk to Me:

"Archangel Chamuel, please fill my heart with love and comfort as I grieve. Help me heal the wounds of loss and nurture the love that remains. Thank you for your soothing presence."

Archangel Samuel

On Grief:

Grief often drains your energy and makes even simple tasks feel overwhelming. I am here to help you restore vitality and process the pain of trauma. Sleep can be a refuge, but I will also guide you toward finding strength and renewal as you heal. Together, we'll embrace life again.

Talk to Me:

"Archangel Samuel, please help me regain vitality and strength as I grieve. Bring me restful sleep and guide me toward healing and renewal. Thank you for your compassionate care."

Archangel Zachariel

On Grief:

Grief can stir destructive tendencies or leave you feeling powerless. I am here to anchor you in strength and guide you through the problems and emotions that arise. Together, we'll replace feelings of helplessness with empowerment, finding solutions and restoring your inner balance.

Talk to Me:

"Archangel Zachariel, please help me navigate the challenges of grief with strength and clarity. Guide me to overcome destructive tendencies and empower me to find balance again. Thank you for your unwavering support."

Archangel Jophiel

On Grief:

Grief often dulls the colors of life, making it hard to see beauty or find gratitude. I bring light to your perception, helping you find moments of grace even in sadness. Together, we'll shift your thoughts toward understanding and gratitude for the love that remains, helping you manifest healing and hope.

Talk to Me:

"Archangel Jophiel, help me see beauty and gratitude even in the midst of my grief. Guide my thoughts toward healing and understanding. Thank you for your uplifting light."

Archangel Laviah

On Grief:

Grief can disconnect you from your intuition, leaving you adrift in sorrow. I bring revelations through dreams and inner wisdom, helping you uncover clarity and connection. Let me guide you to trust the voice within and find peace in the messages of love that still surround you.

LIFE THROUGH ANGEL EYES

Talk to Me:

"Archangel Laviah, guide me through dreams and intuition to find clarity and connection in my grief. Help me trust the wisdom within. Thank you for your gentle guidance."

Archangel Sandalphon

On Grief:

Grief can unground you, leaving you feeling disconnected and overwhelmed. I bring the grounding energy of Earth and the harmony of music to restore balance. Let us find solace in the present moment, where peace and strength reside. Together, we'll replace heaviness with gentle harmony.

Talk to Me:

"Archangel Sandalphon, please help me find grounding and harmony as I grieve. Bring me the solace of music and the peace of balance. Thank you for your steadying presence."

Archangel Jeremiel

On Grief:

Grief is a complex emotion, often tangled with unresolved feelings. I help you reflect with compassion and forgive yourself and others. Together, we'll create a plan for positive change, transforming sorrow into a foundation for healing and hope. The love you've experienced never truly leaves you.

Talk to Me:

"Archangel Jeremiel, guide me in understanding and processing my grief. Help me release unresolved emotions and create a path toward healing and hope. Thank you for your loving guidance."

Archangel Raguel

On Grief:

Grief can create misunderstandings, both with others and within yourself. I am here to harmonize relationships and bring clarity to your inner turmoil. Together, we'll ease the tension grief creates, ensuring that love and understanding remain at the heart of your journey.

Talk to Me:

"Archangel Raguel, please bring harmony and understanding to my relationships and inner struggles during grief. Help me find clarity and peace. Thank you for your gentle care."

Archangel Raziel

On Grief:

Grief often opens a longing for deeper understanding—of the past, the present, and the connections that transcend time. I am here to help you uncover the wisdom of your soul's journey, including past life memories and the spiritual truths that bring comfort and peace.

Talk to Me:

"Archangel Raziel, guide me in understanding the spiritual truths of my grief. Help me uncover the wisdom and connections that bring comfort. Thank you for your enlightening presence."

Archangel Haniel

LIFE THROUGH ANGEL EYES

On Grief:

Grief is often accompanied by frustration and disappointment, as you struggle to find balance after loss. I bring harmony to your heart and mind, helping you navigate the emotional waves with grace. Together, we'll restore equilibrium and replace despair with gentle peace.

Talk to Me:

"Archangel Haniel, help me find balance and harmony as I navigate my grief. Guide me toward peace and emotional stability. Thank you for your compassionate guidance."

ON FEAR

Archangel Michael

On Fear:

Fear can leave you feeling vulnerable and paralyzed, but it is not stronger than your spirit. I am here to shield you from the overwhelming power of fear and help you see clearly. Fear often whispers lies, distorting your perception of yourself and the world. Let me cut through the illusion, strengthening your resolve and guiding you toward courage. Together, we will establish clear boundaries against what threatens your peace, releasing the doubts that fuel your fear.

Talk to Me:

"Archangel Michael, please protect me from the weight of fear and strengthen my courage. Help me release doubt and see clearly, creating boundaries that restore my peace. Thank you for your unwavering support."

Archangel Gabriel

On Fear:

Fear thrives in silence, where unspoken worries and emotions fester. I help you bring those fears to light, expressing them in a way that frees your soul. Communication is a powerful tool to dispel fear, whether through words, creative expression, or sharing your heart with another. Together, we'll replace the heaviness of fear with joy and trust, reminding you that you are capable of overcoming any challenge with clarity and grace.

Talk to Me:

LIFE THROUGH ANGEL EYES

"Archangel Gabriel, help me express my fears so they no longer hold power over me. Guide me to find joy and trust as I move forward. Thank you for your loving guidance."

Archangel Raphael

On Fear:

Fear affects not only the mind but the body as well, manifesting as tension, fatigue, or even illness. I bring healing to the physical and emotional wounds caused by fear, helping you find peace within. Together, we'll uncover the hidden gifts within your fear—lessons of strength, resilience, and love. Let me soothe your heart and guide you toward calm, empowering you to release fear and embrace healing.

Talk to Me:

"Archangel Raphael, please bring healing to my mind, body, and spirit as I release fear. Help me uncover the lessons within and guide me to a place of peace. Thank you for your comforting presence."

Archangel Uriel

On Fear:

Fear often clouds your ability to think clearly, pulling you into despair or uncertainty. I bring wisdom and light to help you navigate fear with clarity and grace. Together, we will face the darkness and transform it into understanding, restoring your inner peace. Fear can also be a doorway to new ideas and perspectives—let me help you see the opportunities hidden within, guiding you toward calm and strength.

Talk to Me:

"Archangel Uriel, please guide me with wisdom and clarity as I face my fears. Help me find peace and uncover the opportunities within the challenges I face. Thank you for your illuminating presence."

Archangel Zadkiel

On Fear:

Fear often stems from unresolved emotions or a lack of forgiveness—for yourself, for others, or even for life itself. I bring calm and compassion to your heart, helping you release the pain that fuels fear. Together, we'll transform fear into discernment, showing you how to trust your inner wisdom. I'll help you find comfort and freedom in forgiveness, allowing you to move forward with peace and clarity.

Talk to Me:

"Archangel Zadkiel, help me release the emotions and pain that fuel my fear. Bring me calm and guide me toward forgiveness, trust, and clarity. Thank you for your gentle care."

Archangel Metatron

On Fear:

Fear can cause you to doubt your worth, making you question your purpose and abilities. I am here to remind you of the divine light within you, a source of courage and truth. Together, we'll reframe fear as a stepping stone to enlightenment, helping you rise above it and step into your power. Let me show you how your fear is a reflection of your desire for growth and transformation.

Talk to Me:

LIFE THROUGH ANGEL EYES

"Archangel Metatron, please help me see fear as a path to growth and enlightenment. Remind me of my divine light and guide me to overcome doubt with courage and truth. Thank you for your wisdom."

Archangel Chamuel

On Fear:

Fear often arises when you feel abandoned or disconnected—from others, from yourself, or from the divine. I bring love and reassurance to help you feel supported and secure, easing the emotional wounds that feed fear. Together, we'll nurture your sense of self-love and inner peace, giving you the strength to face fear with an open heart. You are deeply loved and never alone.

Talk to Me:

"Archangel Chamuel, please fill my heart with love and reassurance as I face my fears. Help me feel supported, secure, and connected to peace. Thank you for your loving presence."

Archangel Samuel

On Fear:

Fear drains your energy and makes you feel stuck, as though life's challenges are too much to bear. I am here to revitalize your spirit and help you face fear with confidence. Together, we'll restore your vitality and guide you to see fear not as a wall but as a step toward strength and renewal. Fear often disrupts sleep and rest, and I'll help you find peace in those moments too.

Talk to Me:

"Archangel Samuel, please restore my energy and confidence as I face fear. Help me find peace in my mind and body so I can move forward with strength. Thank you for your care."

Archangel Zachariel

On Fear:

Fear can stir destructive tendencies or leave you feeling powerless. I bring strength and guidance to help you face these feelings with courage. Together, we'll break down the problems feeding your fear and replace them with solutions and empowerment. Fear can be a sign of where you need to grow, and I'll help you face it head-on.

Talk to Me:

"Archangel Zachariel, help me face fear with courage and guide me toward solutions and empowerment. Bring me the strength to transform fear into growth. Thank you for your steady support."

Archangel Jophiel

On Fear:

Fear often distorts your thoughts, making it hard to see beauty, gratitude, or hope. I bring clarity to your mind, helping you shift your focus away from fear and toward the good that surrounds you. Together, we'll replace unhealthy thoughts with understanding and optimism, allowing you to see the beauty in every challenge.

Talk to Me:

"Archangel Jophiel, help me see beyond fear and focus on the beauty and goodness around me. Guide me to replace unhealthy thoughts with clarity and hope. Thank you for your uplifting light."

LIFE THROUGH ANGEL EYES

Archangel Laviah

On Fear:

Fear clouds your intuition, leaving you disconnected from your inner wisdom. I bring revelations through dreams and insights, helping you understand the roots of your fear. Together, we'll explore the messages your soul is sending, guiding you to trust your intuition and find peace. Fear can't survive in the light of understanding.

Talk to Me:

"Archangel Laviah, guide me through dreams and intuition to uncover the truth behind my fear. Help me trust my inner wisdom and find peace. Thank you for your gentle guidance."

Archangel Sandalphon

On Fear:

Fear can make you feel ungrounded and overwhelmed, as though the world is spinning out of control. I bring the grounding energy of the Earth and the harmony of music to calm your mind. Together, we'll bring balance to your emotions and help you find peace in the present moment.

Talk to Me:

"Archangel Sandalphon, please ground me and calm my fears. Help me find balance through harmony and guide me to peace. Thank you for your steadying presence."

Archangel Jeremiel

On Fear:

Fear often arises from unresolved emotions or a lack of clarity about the future. I help you reflect on the source of your fear and forgive yourself for holding onto it. Together, we'll create a plan for positive change, transforming fear into hope and clarity. Fear can become a tool for growth when viewed through the lens of love.

Talk to Me:

"Archangel Jeremiel, help me understand and release the fear within me. Guide me toward clarity and hope, creating a path of positive change. Thank you for your loving guidance."

Archangel Raguel

On Fear:

Fear often grows from misunderstandings—between yourself and others or between your heart and mind. It clouds your ability to see situations clearly, creating distance where connection is needed most. I bring harmony to dissolve these divides, helping you distinguish between real threats and imagined ones. Together, we will restore your inner confidence, ensuring that fear no longer controls your actions or relationships. Fear can also teach us where healing is needed, and I'll guide you to face it with love and clarity.

Talk to Me:

"Archangel Raguel, please help me understand and dissolve the fears that cloud my mind and heart. Bring harmony to my thoughts and relationships so I may move forward with confidence and peace. Thank you for your guiding care."

Archangel Raziel

On Fear:

LIFE THROUGH ANGEL EYES

Fear can arise from the unknown or from memories buried deep in your soul's journey. I am here to illuminate the shadows and help you uncover the truth behind your fear. Often, fear is tied to lessons from the past, both in this life and beyond. I will guide you to see fear as a doorway to wisdom, a signal pointing to where your spirit seeks growth. Together, we will turn fear into understanding, helping you reclaim your power and step into divine alignment.

Talk to Me:

"Archangel Raziel, help me uncover the spiritual truths and deeper lessons behind my fear. Illuminate the unknown and guide me to transform fear into wisdom and strength. Thank you for your enlightening presence."

Archangel Haniel

On Fear:

Fear disrupts the natural balance within you, creating tension and uncertainty. I bring the energy of harmony to help you face fear with grace and courage. Together, we'll examine the source of your fear and restore emotional alignment, replacing anxiety with trust in yourself and the universe. Fear often stems from disappointment or frustration with life's flow, but I will help you navigate these challenges with patience and faith. You are capable of moving through fear into peace.

Talk to Me:

"Archangel Haniel, please guide me in finding balance and grace as I face my fears. Help me release tension and restore trust in myself and the universe. Thank you for your calming wisdom."

ON ADDICTION

Archangel Michael

On Addiction:

Addiction can feel like a cage, one built from fear, doubt, and a loss of control. I am here to cut through those chains and remind you of your inner strength. Often, addiction arises when you feel powerless, searching for a sense of safety or escape. I will stand by your side, shielding you from harmful influences and empowering you to set clear boundaries. Together, we'll dismantle the patterns that hold you captive and build a foundation of courage and self-respect. Addiction may feel overwhelming, but it is not greater than your spirit.

Talk to Me:

"Archangel Michael, please protect me from the forces of addiction and help me reclaim my strength. Guide me to set clear boundaries and empower me to overcome this challenge. Thank you for standing by my side."

Archangel Gabriel

On Addiction:

Addiction thrives in silence, when emotions go unspoken or creativity is stifled. I help you find your voice, enabling you to express the pain, guilt, or longing that may feed your addiction. Creative expression—whether through writing, music, or speaking your truth—is a powerful way to heal. I bring joy to fill the spaces addiction has claimed, reminding you of the beauty in your authentic self. Together, we'll replace destructive habits with positive outlets for your emotions and energy, allowing you to reconnect with hope and purpose.

Talk to Me:

"Archangel Gabriel, help me express the emotions that fuel my addiction. Guide me toward creative and healing ways to find joy and release guilt. Thank you for your loving encouragement."

Archangel Raphael

On Addiction:

Addiction often signals a deep need for healing—both physical and emotional. I am here to soothe the pain that addiction tries to mask, bringing light to the wounds that need attention. Together, we'll uncover the root causes of your struggle, healing your heart and body with divine love. I will guide you toward practices that restore balance and nurture your well-being, such as meditation, proper nourishment, or energy healing. Addiction is a call for love, and I will help you answer it with compassion for yourself.

Talk to Me:

"Archangel Raphael, please bring healing to the wounds that fuel my addiction. Help me find balance and nurture my body and spirit with love and care. Thank you for your gentle guidance."

Archangel Uriel

On Addiction:

Addiction often grows from feelings of despair, fear, or a lack of purpose. I bring wisdom and clarity to illuminate the underlying pain driving your struggle. Together, we'll confront the shadows of addiction, transforming them into opportunities for growth and peace. I will help you see beyond the immediate cravings or habits, guiding you toward new ideas and positive changes that restore hope. Let me walk with you through the darkness, reminding you of the light within.

Talk to Me:

"Archangel Uriel, help me understand the root of my addiction and guide me toward wisdom and clarity. Show me the path to peace and help me create positive change. Thank you for your illuminating support."

Archangel Zadkiel

On Addiction:

Addiction is often tied to unresolved emotions—anxiety, depression, or guilt—that feel too heavy to bear. I bring calm, comfort, and forgiveness to your heart, helping you release the pain that binds you to unhealthy patterns. Together, we'll replace shame with self-compassion, guiding you to discern the wisdom within your struggle. Addiction does not define you; it is a step on your journey to greater understanding and freedom. I'll help you find peace as you transform your pain into healing.

Talk to Me:

"Archangel Zadkiel, help me release the guilt and pain fueling my addiction. Bring me comfort and forgiveness as I find freedom and healing. Thank you for your compassionate guidance."

Archangel Metatron

On Addiction:

LIFE THROUGH ANGEL EYES

Addiction often distorts your sense of self, making you feel small or unworthy. I am here to remind you of the divine light within you, a limitless source of strength and purpose. Together, we'll reframe addiction as a challenge that awakens your soul, helping you reclaim your self-esteem and spiritual connection. I will guide you to see addiction as an invitation to enlightenment, where each step forward reveals more of your true power. Let me help you replace destructive habits with practices that uplift and inspire you.

Talk to Me:

"Archangel Metatron, please help me reconnect with my divine light and restore my sense of self-worth. Guide me to transform my addiction into a path of enlightenment and growth. Thank you for your empowering presence."

Archangel Chamuel

On Addiction:

Addiction often takes root in feelings of abandonment or a lack of self-love. I bring peace to your heart, nurturing your inner child and soothing the wounds that lead to self-destructive behavior. Together, we'll build a foundation of unconditional love for yourself, helping you break free from the cycles of addiction. I'll guide you to connect with your emotions, replacing impulsive habits with intentional self-care. You are worthy of love, and I am here to help you remember that truth.

Talk to Me:

"Archangel Chamuel, please help me heal the wounds that fuel my addiction and nurture my heart with self-love and peace. Guide me to break free and embrace intentional care for myself. Thank you for your loving presence."

CH JODI M DEHN

Archangel Samuel

On Addiction:

Addiction drains your vitality and disrupts your connection to the restorative power of rest and healing. I bring renewed energy to your body and mind, helping you rebuild the strength to overcome this challenge. Together, we'll address the trauma or pain that addiction seeks to numb, guiding you toward healthy ways of finding peace and renewal. Addiction can feel like a cycle you cannot escape, but I am here to help you reclaim your power and rediscover your purpose.

Talk to Me:

"Archangel Samuel, please restore my energy and help me release the pain fueling my addiction. Guide me to find healthy ways to heal and renew my strength. Thank you for your steady care."

Archangel Zachariel

On Addiction:

Addiction can create destructive tendencies that feel beyond your control, but I bring strength to help you face these challenges. Together, we'll break the problems down into manageable steps, guiding you toward empowerment and freedom. I'll help you uncover the resilience within, replacing harmful patterns with choices that align with your highest good. Addiction may seem overwhelming, but I will walk with you as you reclaim your life.

Talk to Me:

"Archangel Zachariel, help me find the strength to face and overcome my addiction. Guide me to replace destructive tendencies with choices that empower and heal me. Thank you for your steady support."

LIFE THROUGH ANGEL EYES

Archangel Jophiel

On Addiction:

Addiction clouds your thoughts, making it hard to see the beauty and goodness in yourself and your life. I bring clarity to your mind, helping you shift your focus from destructive habits to gratitude and purpose. Together, we'll illuminate the path to healthier choices, reminding you of the beauty within and around you. Addiction does not define you—it's a chance to rediscover the light of hope and understanding.

Talk to Me:

"Archangel Jophiel, please clear the thoughts that bind me to addiction. Help me see the beauty and goodness in my life and guide me to healthier, uplifting choices. Thank you for your inspiring light."

Archangel Laviah

On Addiction:

Addiction often clouds your connection to intuition, leaving you disconnected from the guidance of your soul. I bring revelations through dreams and insight, helping you uncover the underlying emotions and spiritual lessons tied to your addiction. Together, we'll explore the messages your soul is sending, guiding you back to alignment and peace. Addiction cannot hold power over a spirit that trusts its inner wisdom.

Talk to Me:

"Archangel Laviah, guide me through dreams and intuition to uncover the truth behind my addiction. Help me trust my inner wisdom and align with peace. Thank you for your gentle guidance."

CH JODI M DEHN

Archangel Sandalphon

On Addiction:

Addiction can leave you feeling ungrounded and disconnected from your true self. I bring grounding energy to help you find stability and calm in the present moment. Together, we'll replace chaos with harmony, using the power of music and connection to restore balance to your emotions. Addiction can be a call for deeper connection, and I'll help you find it in ways that uplift and inspire you.

Talk to Me:

"Archangel Sandalphon, please ground me and guide me to find harmony and balance as I release my addiction. Help me connect with peace and inspiration. Thank you for your steadying presence."

Archangel Jeremiel

On Addiction:

Addiction often stems from unresolved emotions or a lack of clarity about your path forward. I help you reflect on the patterns fueling your struggle and forgive yourself for past choices. Together, we'll create a plan for positive change, transforming addiction into an opportunity for growth and renewal. Addiction is not the end—it's the beginning of a new chapter filled with hope and purpose.

Talk to Me:

"Archangel Jeremiel, guide me in understanding the patterns behind my addiction and help me forgive myself. Lead me to create positive changes that bring hope and renewal. Thank you for your loving guidance."

LIFE THROUGH ANGEL EYES

Archangel Raguel

On Addiction:

Addiction often thrives on misunderstandings—about yourself, your worth, and your connection to others. I bring harmony to relationships, including the one you have with yourself. Together, we'll repair the fractures caused by addiction, helping you reconnect with trust, love, and accountability. I will guide you to restore balance and mutual understanding in your life, showing you that addiction doesn't define your relationships or your soul. Healing begins with recognizing your inherent worth and the support available to you.

Talk to Me:

"Archangel Raguel, please help me restore balance and harmony in my relationships, including the one with myself. Guide me to rebuild trust and connection as I release addiction. Thank you for your steady presence."

Archangel Raziel

On Addiction:

Addiction often blinds you to the deeper truths about your soul's journey. I help you access the wisdom of past experiences and spiritual lessons to uncover the roots of your struggle. Together, we'll bring clarity to the subconscious patterns driving your addiction, helping you embrace the divine insights waiting within. I'll guide you through dream interpretations, meditations, and intuitive practices that align you with your higher self. Addiction is an obstacle, but it can also be a doorway to profound spiritual transformation.

Talk to Me:

"Archangel Raziel, please help me uncover the spiritual truths behind my addiction. Guide me to interpret the lessons within my soul's journey and align with my higher self. Thank you for your divine insight."

Archangel Haniel

On Addiction:

Addiction often arises from frustration, disappointment, or a lack of inner harmony. I bring balance to your emotions, helping you release the tension that fuels addictive behaviors. Together, we'll restore your sense of peace and remind you of the beauty in balance and moderation. I will help you transform moments of frustration into opportunities for growth and renewal, guiding you to see addiction as a challenge that strengthens your resilience. With harmony restored, you can reconnect with your inner light and purpose.

Talk to Me:

"Archangel Haniel, please bring balance and harmony to my emotions as I release addiction. Guide me to transform frustration into growth and help me find inner peace. Thank you for your calming presence."

ON LACK OF CONFIDENCE

Archangel Michael

On Lack of Confidence:

When confidence falters, it is often fear that whispers doubts into your heart. I am here to help you reclaim your inner strength and stand tall in your truth. Together, we will release the fear that clouds your judgment and dismantle the barriers to self-assurance. Your courage is not lost; it lies waiting for you to rediscover it. Let me shield you from negativity, instill motivation, and remind you that you are capable of far more than you imagine.

Talk to Me:

"Archangel Michael, please strengthen my confidence and shield me from fear and doubt. Help me see my courage and act with assurance. Thank you for your protection and guidance."

Archangel Gabriel

On Lack of Confidence:

Confidence often wavers when your voice feels unheard or your creativity stifled. I will help you express your thoughts, emotions, and ideas with clarity and joy. Together, we'll rebuild your trust in your abilities, especially when it comes to sharing your unique gifts. Confidence comes from embracing who you truly are, and I am here to help you reconnect with your authentic self. Speak, create, and let your light shine—you are worthy of being seen and heard.

Talk to Me:

"Archangel Gabriel, help me find my voice and rebuild my confidence. Guide me to embrace my creativity and express my truth with joy. Thank you for your encouragement."

Archangel Raphael

On Lack of Confidence:

A lack of confidence can be a sign of emotional or spiritual wounds that need healing. I am here to soothe your heart, reminding you of the beauty and strength within you. Together, we'll nurture your spirit and remove the weight of self-doubt. I will guide you to see challenges as opportunities for growth, restoring your faith in yourself. Confidence is not something to seek outside of you—it is a natural part of your being, waiting to be uncovered.

Talk to Me:

"Archangel Raphael, please heal the wounds that hold me back and help me rediscover my inner strength. Guide me to see my worth and move forward with confidence. Thank you for your loving care."

Archangel Uriel

On Lack of Confidence:

A lack of confidence often stems from confusion or fear of the unknown. I bring clarity and wisdom to your heart, helping you understand the deeper causes of your self-doubt. Together, we'll illuminate the path forward, replacing hesitation with trust in your abilities. Confidence grows when you embrace your inner wisdom and recognize your potential. Let me help you find peace and assurance as you navigate this journey.

Talk to Me:

LIFE THROUGH ANGEL EYES

"Archangel Uriel, please bring clarity to my mind and help me overcome the fears that diminish my confidence. Guide me to trust in my inner wisdom and potential. Thank you for your illuminating presence."

Archangel Zadkiel

On Lack of Confidence:

When confidence falters, it can often be traced to lingering feelings of guilt, failure, or inadequacy. I bring forgiveness and calm to your heart, helping you release self-judgment and embrace compassion for yourself. Together, we'll replace self-doubt with wisdom, transforming past mistakes into valuable lessons. You are worthy of confidence and capable of great things. Let me help you see yourself with the same loving eyes I see you with.

Talk to Me:

"Archangel Zadkiel, help me release the guilt and self-doubt that hold me back. Bring calm and wisdom to my heart, guiding me to embrace my worth and move forward with confidence. Thank you for your compassion."

Archangel Metatron

On Lack of Confidence:

Lack of confidence often arises when you forget the divine power within you. I am here to remind you of your limitless potential and your connection to higher truth. Together, we'll reframe challenges as opportunities for growth, empowering you to trust in yourself. Confidence is your birthright, rooted in the light of your soul. Let me guide you to align with that truth, helping you overcome doubt and stand tall in your purpose.

Talk to Me:

"Archangel Metatron, please guide me to reconnect with my divine power and remind me of my limitless potential. Help me trust in myself and walk forward with confidence. Thank you for your empowering light."

Archangel Chamuel

On Lack of Confidence:

Confidence wavers when self-love is forgotten. I am here to nurture your heart, helping you reconnect with the love and compassion you deserve to feel for yourself. Together, we'll heal the inner child who may feel unworthy or abandoned. Confidence grows from a foundation of self-love and acceptance, and I will guide you to embrace both. You are enough, exactly as you are.

Talk to Me:

"Archangel Chamuel, help me nurture my heart and restore my confidence with self-love. Guide me to embrace my worth and move forward with peace and assurance. Thank you for your gentle care."

Archangel Samuel

On Lack of Confidence:

Lack of confidence can stem from exhaustion—emotional, physical, or spiritual. I bring vitality and renewal to your being, helping you rebuild the energy needed to face challenges with assurance. Together, we'll address the root of your doubts and restore your inner strength. Confidence is not about perfection; it's about trusting in your ability to rise.

Talk to Me:

LIFE THROUGH ANGEL EYES

"Archangel Samuel, please restore my energy and renew my confidence. Help me overcome self-doubt and trust in my ability to move forward. Thank you for your steady support."

Archangel Zachariel

On Lack of Confidence:

Confidence often crumbles under the weight of problems or destructive tendencies. I bring strength to help you face challenges head-on, guiding you to see obstacles as stepping stones. Together, we'll break free from limiting beliefs and empower you to embrace your resilience. You are stronger than you know, and I am here to help you realize it.

Talk to Me:

"Archangel Zachariel, help me find the strength to overcome the doubts and challenges that weaken my confidence. Guide me to embrace my resilience and move forward boldly. Thank you for your steadfast guidance."

Archangel Jophiel

On Lack of Confidence:

A lack of confidence often stems from seeing yourself through a distorted lens. I bring beauty and clarity to your thoughts, helping you recognize your inherent worth and potential. Together, we'll shift your focus from self-doubt to gratitude, replacing insecurity with understanding and self-acceptance. Confidence is about seeing yourself as you truly are—magnificent and capable.

Talk to Me:

"Archangel Jophiel, please bring clarity to my mind and help me see myself with love and appreciation. Guide me to embrace my worth and move forward with confidence. Thank you for your illuminating presence."

Archangel Laviah

On Lack of Confidence:

Confidence falters when intuition is ignored or hidden truths remain buried. I bring revelations to help you understand the roots of your doubts and guide you to trust your inner voice. Together, we'll uncover the wisdom within and align you with your higher self. Confidence grows when you honor your intuition and embrace your unique path.

Talk to Me:

"Archangel Laviah, help me uncover the truths that block my confidence and guide me to trust my intuition. Bring clarity and alignment to my spirit. Thank you for your gentle guidance."

Archangel Sandalphon

On Lack of Confidence:

Confidence often fades when you feel ungrounded or disconnected. I bring grounding energy to help you find stability and reconnect with your purpose. Together, we'll harmonize your emotions and replace doubt with calm assurance. Music and creative expression can anchor you in the present, reminding you of your unique gifts and worth.

Talk to Me:

LIFE THROUGH ANGEL EYES

"Archangel Sandalphon, please ground me and help me find balance as I rebuild my confidence. Guide me to trust in my purpose and reconnect with my inner strength. Thank you for your steady presence."

Archangel Jeremiel

On Lack of Confidence:

A lack of confidence often stems from unresolved emotions or unacknowledged successes. I help you reflect on your journey, showing you the strength and victories you may have overlooked. Together, we'll create a plan for growth and renewal, reminding you that confidence is built one step at a time. Trust your journey—you're exactly where you're meant to be.

Talk to Me:

"Archangel Jeremiel, help me reflect on my journey and recognize the strength within me. Guide me to create a plan for growth and move forward with confidence. Thank you for your loving support."

Archangel Raguel

On Lack of Confidence:

Confidence often falters when misunderstandings—especially within yourself—cloud your vision. I bring harmony and clarity to your heart, helping you rebuild trust in your own abilities. Together, we'll resolve the inner conflicts that fuel your self-doubt, creating a foundation of self-respect and assurance. You are capable, and I am here to remind you of that truth.

Talk to Me:

"Archangel Raguel, help me bring harmony to the inner conflicts that weaken my confidence. Guide me to rebuild trust in myself and my abilities. Thank you for your steady guidance."

Archangel Raziel

On Lack of Confidence:

Confidence fades when you lose sight of the divine wisdom and strength within you. I help you access the hidden knowledge of your soul, unlocking the lessons from your past and the spiritual truths guiding your journey. Together, we'll uncover the deeper reasons behind your lack of confidence and transform self-doubt into clarity and purpose. Confidence arises when you embrace your connection to the divine and trust in your soul's path. Let me show you how your unique experiences have prepared you to shine brightly.

Talk to Me:

"Archangel Raziel, help me uncover the spiritual truths behind my lack of confidence. Guide me to trust in my soul's wisdom and embrace the divine strength within me. Thank you for your enlightening presence."

Archangel Haniel

On Lack of Confidence:

Confidence often diminishes when you feel out of harmony with yourself or the world around you. I bring balance and tranquility to your emotions, helping you overcome feelings of inadequacy or disappointment. Together, we'll restore the delicate balance between your heart and mind, reminding you of your unique gifts and inner light. Confidence flourishes when you trust in your natural rhythms

LIFE THROUGH ANGEL EYES

and align with the harmony of life. I will guide you to rediscover your inner beauty and walk with grace.

Talk to Me:

"Archangel Haniel, please bring balance to my emotions and help me restore harmony within myself. Guide me to see my worth and move forward with confidence and grace. Thank you for your gentle wisdom."

ON UNDERSTANDING

Archangel Michael

On Understanding:

True understanding begins with courage—the courage to face truths about yourself and the world around you. I will help you cut through confusion and fear to see with clarity and conviction. Together, we will dismantle the barriers preventing you from embracing a deeper awareness. When you release doubt and trust in your ability to comprehend, the light of understanding will guide you.

Talk to Me:

"Archangel Michael, help me clear away fear and confusion, granting me the courage to see truth and deepen my understanding. Thank you for your strength and guidance."

Archangel Gabriel

On Understanding:

Understanding blooms when communication flows freely. Whether it's expressing yourself or receiving wisdom from others, I'll guide you to connect with clarity and empathy. I'll also help you understand the role of joy and creativity in expanding your perspective. Together, we'll craft a path where understanding becomes an open channel between you and the divine.

Talk to Me:

"Archangel Gabriel, help me communicate with clarity and empathy, guiding me to deeper understanding in all areas of my life. Thank you for your nurturing wisdom."

LIFE THROUGH ANGEL EYES

Archangel Raphael

On Understanding:

Understanding often requires healing—healing of old wounds or misconceptions. I will soothe your heart and clear away the emotional and spiritual blocks that hinder your comprehension. Together, we'll find the deeper lessons hidden in your experiences, helping you see life through the lens of compassion and wholeness.

Talk to Me:

"Archangel Raphael, please heal the wounds that cloud my perspective, and guide me to understanding through compassion and clarity. Thank you for your loving presence."

Archangel Uriel

On Understanding:

Understanding requires wisdom, and wisdom often comes through illuminating the shadows of confusion. I am here to shed light on the unknown, helping you make sense of difficult emotions or complex situations. Together, we'll replace fear with clarity, leading you to profound insights and peace.

Talk to Me:

"Archangel Uriel, bring light to the shadows of my confusion, guiding me to deep understanding and peace. Thank you for your wisdom and illumination."

Archangel Zadkiel

On Understanding:

True understanding requires forgiveness—of yourself, others, and the circumstances that shaped you. I help you release judgment and embrace compassion, creating space for wisdom to flow. Together, we'll quiet the mind and open your heart, showing you how understanding and forgiveness are intertwined.

Talk to Me:

"Archangel Zadkiel, help me release judgment and open my heart to forgiveness, guiding me to profound understanding. Thank you for your compassionate wisdom."

Archangel Metatron

On Understanding:

Understanding expands when you connect with higher truths. I will help you access divine wisdom and align with the greater purpose behind your challenges. Together, we'll organize the chaos of your thoughts, empowering you to see the bigger picture. True understanding lies in recognizing your place in the infinite tapestry of creation.

Talk to Me:

"Archangel Metatron, guide me to higher truths and help me see the greater purpose in my journey. Thank you for your enlightening presence."

Archangel Chamuel

On Understanding:

Understanding begins with love—for yourself, others, and the world. I help you see the beauty in connection and the lessons within every experience. Together, we'll explore the emotional truths that deepen your understanding and heal the bonds that confusion or doubt may have strained. Let love be your compass.

Talk to Me:

"Archangel Chamuel, guide me to understanding through love and help me see the beauty and lessons in every connection. Thank you for your gentle guidance."

Archangel Samuel

On Understanding:

Understanding is often clouded by exhaustion or trauma. I bring vitality and renewal, helping you find the energy to approach situations with fresh perspective. Together, we'll clear the fog of confusion, empowering you to embrace clarity and a renewed sense of awareness.

Talk to Me:

"Archangel Samuel, please restore my energy and help me approach life with clarity and understanding. Thank you for your revitalizing presence."

Archangel Zachariel

On Understanding:

When problems feel overwhelming, understanding can feel out of reach. I bring strength and patience, helping you untangle complexity and find the wisdom hidden within struggles. Together, we'll break down barriers to understanding, guiding you to see challenges as opportunities for growth.

Talk to Me:

"Archangel Zachariel, help me find the strength and patience to understand the challenges in my life. Thank you for your steadfast guidance."

Archangel Jophiel

On Understanding:

Understanding blossoms when you see the beauty in all things, including the difficulties. I help you shift your perspective, finding gratitude and wisdom where there was once confusion. Together, we'll reframe your thoughts, showing you how every moment holds a lesson waiting to be understood.

Talk to Me:

"Archangel Jophiel, help me see the beauty and lessons in all things, guiding me to deeper understanding and gratitude. Thank you for your illuminating love."

Archangel Laviah

On Understanding:

Revelation is the foundation of understanding. I guide you to access your intuition and uncover truths hidden in your subconscious. Together, we'll explore the dreams and insights that can reveal what you seek to understand. Trust in your inner wisdom; it's waiting to guide you.

Talk to Me:

"Archangel Laviah, guide me to the revelations that will deepen my understanding and help me trust in my intuition. Thank you for your gentle insights."

LIFE THROUGH ANGEL EYES

Archangel Sandalphon

On Understanding:

Understanding comes when you're grounded in the present. I bring calm and stability to your heart, helping you approach situations with clarity and focus. Through music or creative expression, you can uncover insights and harmonize your emotions, leading to greater understanding of yourself and others.

Talk to Me:

"Archangel Sandalphon, ground me in the present and guide me to understanding through harmony and calm. Thank you for your steady support."

Archangel Jeremiel

On Understanding:

Understanding often requires reflection. I help you review your journey with clarity, showing you how past experiences have shaped your present. Together, we'll create a plan for positive change, helping you gain deeper insights and move forward with wisdom and purpose.

Talk to Me:

"Archangel Jeremiel, guide me to reflect on my journey and find the understanding I need to move forward with clarity. Thank you for your loving support."

Archangel Raguel

On Understanding:

Misunderstandings often create barriers to deeper connections. I bring harmony and balance, helping you see through the lens of empathy and truth. Together, we'll mend relationships and restore the understanding that leads to peace. Trust that unity begins with clarity and compassion.

Talk to Me:

"Archangel Raguel, help me see through the lens of empathy and restore harmony in my relationships and within myself. Thank you for your guiding presence."

Archangel Raziel

On Understanding:

Understanding often lies in hidden knowledge and spiritual truths. I help you access the deeper meanings behind your experiences, guiding you to trust in the divine plan. Together, we'll uncover the mysteries that lead to clarity and purpose, showing you how understanding connects you to the infinite wisdom of the universe.

Talk to Me:

"Archangel Raziel, guide me to the hidden truths and deeper understanding of my journey. Thank you for your enlightening guidance."

Archangel Haniel

On Understanding:

Understanding thrives in harmony. I bring balance to your emotions, helping you find clarity in moments of frustration or doubt. Together, we'll restore your inner calm, allowing you to approach life

LIFE THROUGH ANGEL EYES

with grace and insight. Understanding begins when you trust in the natural rhythm of your soul's journey.

Talk to Me:

"Archangel Haniel, help me find balance and harmony, guiding me to approach life with grace and understanding. Thank you for your gentle wisdom."

ON DISCERNMENT

Archangel Michael

On Discernment:

Discernment is the ability to see clearly through the fog of doubt and deception. I bring clarity and strength to your decisions, helping you separate truth from illusion. When you ask for my guidance, I will cut away distractions and fears, leaving only what serves your highest good. Trust that with my help, you can stand firm in your decisions and follow the path of integrity.

Talk to Me:

"Archangel Michael, help me see through illusions and strengthen my ability to make clear, truthful decisions. Thank you for your protective guidance."

Archangel Gabriel

On Discernment:

Discernment flourishes through communication—both with yourself and with others. I help you tune into your inner voice and express your truth with confidence. I will guide you to recognize genuine intentions, whether in your own heart or in those around you. Together, we'll foster a deeper connection to your intuition and wisdom.

Talk to Me:

"Archangel Gabriel, guide me to listen to my inner voice and communicate with clarity, helping me discern truth and act with confidence. Thank you for your nurturing wisdom."

LIFE THROUGH ANGEL EYES

Archangel Raphael

On Discernment:

Discernment is a healing process, as it often involves letting go of what no longer serves you. I will help you release unhealthy patterns and see situations with compassion and clarity. Together, we'll remove emotional and spiritual clutter, allowing you to make decisions that promote your well-being and growth.

Talk to Me:

"Archangel Raphael, help me release what no longer serves me and guide me to discern the choices that support my healing and growth. Thank you for your loving care."

Archangel Uriel

On Discernment:

Discernment is born from wisdom and light. I illuminate the path before you, helping you understand the deeper implications of your choices. I will guide you to make decisions rooted in peace, clarity, and divine insight. Trust in my light to help you navigate complexity with confidence.

Talk to Me:

"Archangel Uriel, illuminate my path and guide me to make wise and peaceful decisions. Thank you for your enlightening presence."

Archangel Zadkiel

On Discernment:

Discernment often requires compassion and forgiveness. I help you release judgment and see through the lens of wisdom and understanding. Together, we'll cultivate a calm and balanced mind, enabling you to make decisions with clarity and grace, free from the weight of fear or guilt.

Talk to Me:

"Archangel Zadkiel, guide me to discern with wisdom and compassion, helping me make choices aligned with my highest good. Thank you for your calming guidance."

Archangel Metatron

On Discernment:

Discernment thrives in clarity and structure. I help you organize your thoughts and align with divine truths. Together, we'll clear the mental chaos that clouds your judgment, empowering you to make decisions that resonate with your spiritual purpose. Trust in the higher perspective I bring to your life.

Talk to Me:

"Archangel Metatron, help me organize my thoughts and align with divine wisdom, guiding me to make decisions with clarity and purpose. Thank you for your enlightening insight."

Archangel Chamuel

On Discernment:

Discernment begins in the heart. I help you tune into your emotions and recognize what resonates with love and peace. Whether you're making decisions about relationships or life paths, I will guide you to discern what nurtures your soul and let go of what causes harm.

Talk to Me:

LIFE THROUGH ANGEL EYES

"Archangel Chamuel, guide me to discern with love and peace, helping me choose the paths and connections that nurture my heart. Thank you for your gentle guidance."

Archangel Samuel

On Discernment:

Discernment requires energy and focus. When fatigue clouds your judgment, I bring vitality to restore your clarity and perspective. Together, we'll ensure you have the strength to make mindful choices and navigate life's challenges with resilience and wisdom.

Talk to Me:

"Archangel Samuel, restore my energy and guide me to discern with clarity and focus. Thank you for your revitalizing presence."

Archangel Zachariel

On Discernment:

Discernment often involves overcoming destructive tendencies and recognizing your inner strength. I help you see beyond impulsive reactions or habits, empowering you to make choices rooted in courage and wisdom. Trust in your ability to face challenges with clarity and resolve.

Talk to Me:

"Archangel Zachariel, help me recognize my strength and guide me to discern with courage and wisdom. Thank you for your steadfast support."

Archangel Jophiel

On Discernment:

Discernment is about seeing the beauty in truth. I help you shift your perspective, showing you how clarity and understanding can bring peace to your life. Together, we'll illuminate the path of gratitude and self-awareness, helping you make decisions that align with your highest aspirations.

Talk to Me:

"Archangel Jophiel, guide me to see the beauty and truth in every decision, helping me discern with grace and clarity. Thank you for your uplifting guidance."

Archangel Laviah

On Discernment:

Discernment often comes through dreams and intuition. I guide you to trust your inner wisdom and interpret the subtle messages of your subconscious. Together, we'll uncover the truths that lie hidden within, empowering you to make decisions with confidence and insight.

Talk to Me:

"Archangel Laviah, guide me to trust my intuition and reveal the truths I need to discern wisely. Thank you for your gentle insights."

Archangel Sandalphon

On Discernment:

Discernment grows when you are grounded in the present moment. I help you calm your mind and emotions, creating space for clarity to emerge. Whether through music or quiet reflection, I will guide you to connect with your inner wisdom and choose with confidence and peace.

LIFE THROUGH ANGEL EYES

Talk to Me:

"Archangel Sandalphon, help me ground myself in the present and guide me to discern with clarity and peace. Thank you for your calming presence."

Archangel Jeremiel

On Discernment:

Discernment is the result of reflection and clarity. I help you review your past decisions and learn from them, guiding you to choose wisely for the future. Together, we'll bring clarity to your intentions, enabling you to plan for positive change with confidence and understanding.

Talk to Me:

"Archangel Jeremiel, guide me to reflect on my past and discern with clarity, helping me plan for a brighter future. Thank you for your loving support."

Archangel Raguel

On Discernment:

Discernment is essential in navigating relationships and resolving misunderstandings. I bring harmony and fairness, helping you recognize genuine intentions and make decisions that foster peace. Together, we'll create a foundation of trust and clarity in your interactions with others.

Talk to Me:

"Archangel Raguel, help me discern with fairness and clarity, fostering harmony in my relationships. Thank you for your balanced guidance."

Archangel Raziel

On Discernment:

Discernment often involves understanding the deeper, spiritual truths of life. I help you access divine wisdom and see beyond surface appearances. Together, we'll uncover the hidden meanings behind your experiences, empowering you to choose paths aligned with your soul's purpose.

Talk to Me:

"Archangel Raziel, guide me to the deeper truths and help me discern with wisdom and clarity. Thank you for your enlightening guidance."

Archangel Haniel

On Discernment:

Discernment thrives in balance and harmony. I bring peace to your emotions, helping you navigate choices with grace and confidence. Together, we'll align your intuition and reason, ensuring that your decisions reflect the natural rhythm of your life's journey.

Talk to Me:

"Archangel Haniel, help me find balance and guide me to discern with grace and harmony. Thank you for your gentle wisdom."

ON GRATITUDE

Archangel Michael

On Gratitude:

Gratitude is a shield of light that repels fear and doubt. When you acknowledge the blessings in your life, even during challenges, you summon divine protection and strength. I help you see the courage within you and recognize the moments of grace that sustain you. Gratitude for your journey builds the resilience to overcome any obstacle.

Talk to Me:

"Archangel Michael, help me cultivate gratitude for my journey and see the strength in my challenges. Thank you for your protective presence."

Archangel Gabriel

On Gratitude:

Gratitude is the language of joy. When you express thankfulness, you invite harmony into your life. I guide you to communicate appreciation—both to yourself and others—and to celebrate the beauty in every moment. Gratitude unlocks creativity and opens the path to divine inspiration. Let it flow freely through your words and actions.

Talk to Me:

"Archangel Gabriel, guide me to express gratitude with joy and clarity, helping me appreciate the beauty in all things. Thank you for your inspiring guidance."

Archangel Raphael

On Gratitude:

Gratitude is a powerful healing force. When you shift your focus to the blessings in your life, your heart begins to mend, and your spirit feels renewed. I help you recognize the gifts hidden in every experience, even in pain. Together, we'll turn your focus toward gratitude, inviting profound healing into your life.

Talk to Me:

"Archangel Raphael, guide me to find gratitude in every experience, and heal my heart with the power of appreciation. Thank you for your loving care."

Archangel Uriel

On Gratitude:

Gratitude is the foundation of wisdom. When you give thanks, you gain clarity about life's purpose and the interconnectedness of all things. I illuminate your path, showing you how gratitude transforms despair into hope and confusion into understanding. Together, we'll cultivate a grateful heart that radiates peace and wisdom.

Talk to Me:

"Archangel Uriel, help me see the wisdom in gratitude and guide me to a heart filled with peace and clarity. Thank you for your enlightening presence."

Archangel Zadkiel

On Gratitude:

LIFE THROUGH ANGEL EYES

Gratitude is a key to forgiveness. By appreciating the lessons in your journey, you release resentment and open your heart to peace. I help you find gratitude even in life's challenges, teaching you to see the beauty in every moment. Together, we'll transform your perspective, bringing calm and comfort to your soul.

Talk to Me:

"Archangel Zadkiel, help me find gratitude in all circumstances and guide me to a heart filled with peace and forgiveness. Thank you for your gentle wisdom."

Archangel Metatron

On Gratitude:

Gratitude elevates your vibration, connecting you to the divine. When you recognize the blessings in your life, you align with the greater truths of the universe. I help you organize your thoughts and focus on what truly matters. Together, we'll amplify your gratitude, unlocking your potential for growth and enlightenment.

Talk to Me:

"Archangel Metatron, guide me to focus on gratitude and align with divine truths. Thank you for helping me grow and ascend with clarity."

Archangel Chamuel

On Gratitude:

Gratitude nurtures love and connection. When you appreciate the people and experiences in your life, you strengthen the bonds of your relationships. I help you open your heart to gratitude, fostering self-love and healing emotional wounds. Together, we'll create a space for love and peace to flourish.

Talk to Me:

"Archangel Chamuel, guide me to open my heart to gratitude and strengthen the love within and around me. Thank you for your gentle guidance."

Archangel Samuel

On Gratitude:

Gratitude restores energy and vitality. By focusing on the blessings in your life, you can shift from exhaustion to renewal. I guide you to find moments of thankfulness even in the mundane, reigniting your spirit and filling you with purpose. Together, we'll cultivate a grateful heart full of energy and hope.

Talk to Me:

"Archangel Samuel, help me find gratitude in all aspects of life and restore my energy with thankfulness. Thank you for your revitalizing presence."

Archangel Zachariel

On Gratitude:

Gratitude strengthens your inner resilience. Even in the face of challenges, finding reasons to be thankful builds your resolve and courage. I guide you to recognize the blessings hidden in struggles, helping you rise with renewed determination. Together, we'll transform hardships into opportunities for growth through the power of gratitude.

LIFE THROUGH ANGEL EYES

Talk to Me:

"Archangel Zachariel, help me find strength through gratitude and guide me to embrace challenges as opportunities. Thank you for your steadfast support."

Archangel Jophiel

On Gratitude:

Gratitude opens your eyes to the beauty of life. I help you see the blessings in every situation, shifting your perspective from lack to abundance. Together, we'll focus on the small joys that brighten your day, reminding you of the beauty that surrounds and uplifts you.

Talk to Me:

"Archangel Jophiel, guide me to see the beauty and blessings in my life, cultivating a heart filled with gratitude. Thank you for your illuminating presence."

Archangel Laviah

On Gratitude:

Gratitude often reveals itself through quiet reflection. I guide you to connect with your inner wisdom and uncover the blessings hidden within your journey. Together, we'll explore the dreams and insights that inspire thankfulness, showing you how gratitude aligns you with your soul's purpose.

Talk to Me:

"Archangel Laviah, help me reflect and uncover the blessings in my journey, guiding me to a heart full of gratitude. Thank you for your gentle insight."

CH JODI M DEHN

Archangel Sandalphon

On Gratitude:

Gratitude resonates with the harmony of the universe. Through music, prayer, or stillness, I help you connect with this universal rhythm, inspiring thankfulness for every moment. Together, we'll cultivate a grounded, grateful heart that embraces the joy and balance of life.

Talk to Me:

"Archangel Sandalphon, guide me to resonate with gratitude and embrace the harmony of life. Thank you for your grounding presence."

Archangel Jeremiel

On Gratitude:

Gratitude often comes from reflecting on your journey. I help you review your life with clarity, showing you how each experience has shaped and blessed you. Together, we'll uncover the reasons to be thankful, empowering you to move forward with a heart full of hope and appreciation.

Talk to Me:

"Archangel Jeremiel, guide me to reflect on my journey and find gratitude in my experiences. Thank you for your loving guidance."

Archangel Raguel

On Gratitude:

Gratitude brings harmony to relationships. When you express appreciation for others, you strengthen the bonds of understanding and peace. I help you foster gratitude in your interactions, ensuring fairness and balance in all your connections. Together, we'll create a foundation of mutual respect and thankfulness.

Talk to Me:

"Archangel Raguel, help me cultivate gratitude in my relationships and guide me to foster harmony and peace. Thank you for your balanced guidance."

Archangel Raziel

On Gratitude:

Gratitude is a key to unlocking spiritual wisdom. When you give thanks, you align with the divine energy that connects all things. I help you see the deeper truths in your blessings, guiding you to appreciate the infinite wisdom of the universe. Together, we'll deepen your spiritual understanding through gratitude.

Talk to Me:

"Archangel Raziel, guide me to see the divine truths in my blessings and deepen my gratitude for life's mysteries. Thank you for your enlightening presence."

Archangel Haniel

On Gratitude:

Gratitude flows when your heart is in balance. I help you harmonize your emotions, opening your heart to thankfulness and grace. Together, we'll embrace the gentle rhythm of life, showing you how gratitude brings serenity and joy to every moment.

Talk to Me:

CH JODI M DEHN

"Archangel Haniel, guide me to harmonize my heart and embrace gratitude with grace. Thank you for your calming wisdom."

ON EMPTY NEST

Archangel Michael

On Empty Nest:

The empty nest is a new chapter, one that can feel both freeing and uncertain. I am here to protect you from the fears that arise in this transition. Let me guide you to rediscover your inner strength and purpose, helping you embrace this time as an opportunity for personal growth. Trust that the love you've given to your family continues to flourish, even as the house quiets.

Talk to Me:

"Archangel Michael, guide me through this transition with courage and protect me from fear as I embrace this new chapter. Thank you for your steadfast strength."

Archangel Gabriel

On Empty Nest:

The empty nest brings the chance to find new ways to express yourself. Whether through creative pursuits, deeper communication with loved ones, or exploring your own dreams, I am here to inspire you. Let me help you find joy in this space, as you write the next chapter of your life.

Talk to Me:

"Archangel Gabriel, inspire me to express myself with creativity and joy as I navigate this transition. Thank you for your nurturing guidance."

Archangel Raphael

On Empty Nest:

This time can bring emotions to the surface, some of which may feel like loss. I am here to soothe your heart and help you heal from any sadness. Together, we'll focus on the blessings this change offers, finding renewal and well-being in this next stage of life.

Talk to Me:

"Archangel Raphael, heal my heart and guide me to embrace the blessings of this new chapter with peace and renewal. Thank you for your loving care."

Archangel Uriel

On Empty Nest:

Transitions like the empty nest are a time to seek wisdom and understanding. I bring light to your path, helping you find peace in this change and clarity about the opportunities ahead. Trust that this shift is part of your life's divine plan, and I'll guide you toward new ideas and purpose.

Talk to Me:

"Archangel Uriel, bring wisdom and peace to my heart as I adjust to this new stage of life. Thank you for your enlightening presence."

Archangel Zadkiel

On Empty Nest:

The empty nest can stir emotions like loneliness or regret. I help you find forgiveness for yourself and others, guiding you to release

LIFE THROUGH ANGEL EYES

these feelings and find comfort. Together, we'll focus on the joy and wisdom you've gained and the new opportunities that await.

Talk to Me:

"Archangel Zadkiel, guide me to release regret and embrace this new chapter with comfort and forgiveness. Thank you for your calming support."

Archangel Metatron

On Empty Nest:

The empty nest is a time to reconnect with your divine purpose. I help you organize your thoughts and focus on what you want to create in this next phase of your life. Together, we'll unlock your potential for personal growth and spiritual ascension.

Talk to Me:

"Archangel Metatron, help me align with my divine purpose and focus on new possibilities. Thank you for your enlightening guidance."

Archangel Chamuel

On Empty Nest:

The quiet of an empty nest can make you feel disconnected, but it's also a chance to deepen self-love and emotional healing. I help you nurture your inner child, fostering peace and self-compassion. Together, we'll create a life filled with love and harmony in this new chapter.

Talk to Me:

"Archangel Chamuel, guide me to nurture self-love and find peace in the stillness of this transition. Thank you for your tender guidance."

Archangel Samuel

On Empty Nest:

The empty nest can leave you feeling drained or uncertain, but it's also a time to rejuvenate. I bring vitality and clarity, helping you rediscover your energy and sense of purpose. Together, we'll focus on creating a life that inspires and fulfills you.

Talk to Me:

"Archangel Samuel, restore my energy and guide me to find purpose and renewal in this new phase of life. Thank you for your revitalizing support."

Archangel Zachariel

On Empty Nest:

The empty nest can bring challenges, but it also highlights your inner strength. I help you overcome feelings of loss and find resilience in this transition. Together, we'll uncover new opportunities for growth and fulfillment, proving that this is not an end but a new beginning.

Talk to Me:

"Archangel Zachariel, help me find strength and resilience as I embrace the possibilities of this new stage. Thank you for your unwavering support."

Archangel Jophiel

On Empty Nest:

LIFE THROUGH ANGEL EYES

The empty nest is an opportunity to see the beauty in change. I help you shift your perspective to appreciate the blessings of this stage—more time for yourself, new experiences, and personal growth. Together, we'll celebrate the beauty of life's ever-changing journey.

Talk to Me:

"Archangel Jophiel, guide me to see the beauty and blessings in this transition. Thank you for your uplifting presence."

Archangel Laviah

On Empty Nest:

The quiet of an empty nest is a powerful time for reflection. I help you explore the dreams and insights you may have set aside, guiding you to rediscover your inner wisdom. Together, we'll find clarity and inspiration for this new chapter of your life.

Talk to Me:

"Archangel Laviah, guide me to reflect deeply and rediscover my dreams in the stillness of this new stage. Thank you for your gentle insight."

Archangel Sandalphon

On Empty Nest:

The quiet of an empty nest allows you to reconnect with the rhythms of your life. Through music, prayer, or meditation, I help you ground yourself and find harmony in this new stage. Together, we'll create a sense of peace and balance that nourishes your soul.

Talk to Me:

"Archangel Sandalphon, guide me to find balance and harmony in the quiet of this transition. Thank you for your grounding presence."

Archangel Jeremiel

On Empty Nest:

The empty nest is a time to reflect on all you've accomplished and plan for a positive future. I guide you to review your life with clarity and gratitude, helping you see how far you've come. Together, we'll create a vision for a joyful, fulfilling new chapter.

Talk to Me:

"Archangel Jeremiel, guide me to reflect on my journey with gratitude and plan for a fulfilling future. Thank you for your loving guidance."

Archangel Raguel

On Empty Nest:

The empty nest often involves redefining relationships—with your children, your partner, and yourself. I bring harmony and balance, helping you navigate these shifts with fairness and understanding. Together, we'll foster connections that honor your needs and those of your loved ones.

Talk to Me:

"Archangel Raguel, guide me to create harmony in my relationships and embrace the balance of this new phase. Thank you for your supportive wisdom."

Archangel Raziel

On Empty Nest:

LIFE THROUGH ANGEL EYES

The empty nest is a time to explore the deeper, spiritual aspects of your life. I guide you to uncover the hidden wisdom and truths within you, helping you see this transition as an opportunity for self-discovery. Together, we'll align your soul's purpose with this new chapter.

Talk to Me:

"Archangel Raziel, guide me to uncover the spiritual truths of this new phase and align with my soul's purpose. Thank you for your enlightening insight."

Archangel Haniel

On Empty Nest:

The empty nest requires balance and harmony to navigate its emotional waves. I help you find peace in your heart and restore equilibrium as you embrace this time of change. Together, we'll cultivate a life of grace and fulfillment that honors your journey.

Talk to Me:

"Archangel Haniel, help me find balance and peace as I navigate the emotions of this transition. Thank you for your calming wisdom."

ON RELATIONSHIP CONFLICTS

Archangel Michael

On Relationship Conflicts:

Conflict can feel like a battlefield, but it's also an opportunity to establish clear boundaries and protect what matters most—your peace and integrity. I help you stand strong in your truth without falling into fear or anger. Together, we'll cut through negativity and create space for resolution and understanding.

Talk to Me:

"Archangel Michael, guide me to stand strong in my truth and help me resolve conflict with clarity and peace. Thank you for your protective strength."

Archangel Gabriel

On Relationship Conflicts:

Communication is the heart of resolution. I help you speak with honesty, compassion, and clarity so that your words foster connection rather than division. Together, we'll find a way to express your needs while understanding the perspectives of others, turning discord into harmony.

Talk to Me:

"Archangel Gabriel, guide my words to be compassionate and clear so I may foster connection and resolution. Thank you for your inspiring guidance."

Archangel Raphael

LIFE THROUGH ANGEL EYES

On Relationship Conflicts:

Conflict often stems from unresolved pain or misunderstandings. I help heal the emotional wounds that fuel discord, opening hearts to forgiveness and empathy. Together, we'll soothe the tension, promoting emotional healing for you and those involved.

Talk to Me:

"Archangel Raphael, heal the pain underlying this conflict and guide me to bring compassion and peace to my relationships. Thank you for your loving care."

Archangel Uriel

On Relationship Conflicts:

Conflict clouds your judgment and stirs emotions. I bring light to the situation, helping you see the truth with clarity and wisdom. Together, we'll find solutions rooted in understanding and transform fear or anger into peaceful resolution.

Talk to Me:

"Archangel Uriel, bring clarity and wisdom to this conflict so I may approach it with understanding and peace. Thank you for your enlightening presence."

Archangel Zadkiel

On Relationship Conflicts:

Forgiveness is the key to resolving conflict. I help you let go of resentment and embrace understanding, even when it feels challenging. Together, we'll transform the energy of conflict into compassion, restoring harmony and trust in your relationships.

Talk to Me:

"Archangel Zadkiel, guide me to forgive and find compassion so I may resolve conflict with grace. Thank you for your gentle wisdom."

Archangel Metatron

On Relationship Conflicts:

Relationships are sacred spaces for growth and learning. Conflict can highlight areas that need attention and alignment. I help you organize your thoughts, focus on solutions, and approach disagreements with a higher perspective. Together, we'll transform tension into an opportunity for spiritual and emotional growth.

Talk to Me:

"Archangel Metatron, guide me to approach conflict with clarity and a higher perspective. Thank you for helping me align my relationships with divine purpose."

Archangel Chamuel

On Relationship Conflicts:

Conflict can create a sense of abandonment or disconnection. I help you nurture the love within your heart, healing emotional wounds and restoring peace. Together, we'll address the root of the conflict, fostering understanding and harmony in your relationships.

Talk to Me:

"Archangel Chamuel, help me heal emotional wounds and restore harmony in my relationships. Thank you for your tender guidance."

Archangel Samuel

LIFE THROUGH ANGEL EYES

On Relationship Conflicts:

Conflict can drain your energy, but it also provides a chance to revitalize the connection. I bring clarity and focus, helping you navigate disagreements with grace and rebuild vitality in your relationships. Together, we'll create a foundation for stronger, more harmonious bonds.

Talk to Me:

"Archangel Samuel, guide me to restore energy and strengthen my relationships as we resolve conflicts. Thank you for your revitalizing support."

Archangel Zachariel

On Relationship Conflicts:

Conflict tests your inner strength and patience. I help you face these challenges with resilience and the courage to address issues directly. Together, we'll turn difficulties into opportunities for deeper understanding and stronger connections.

Talk to Me:

"Archangel Zachariel, help me approach conflicts with strength and transform them into opportunities for growth. Thank you for your unwavering support."

Archangel Jophiel

On Relationship Conflicts:

Even in conflict, there is beauty to be found—lessons to learn and growth to embrace. I help you shift your perspective, focusing on the positive aspects of your relationships and the potential for resolution. Together, we'll find gratitude and understanding in even the most challenging moments.

Talk to Me:

"Archangel Jophiel, guide me to see the beauty and growth in my relationships, even during conflict. Thank you for your illuminating presence."

Archangel Laviah

On Relationship Conflicts:

Conflict often arises from miscommunication or unspoken truths. I help you connect with your intuition to uncover the deeper issues at play. Together, we'll bring clarity to the situation, guiding you to resolve misunderstandings with wisdom and grace.

Talk to Me:

"Archangel Laviah, guide me to uncover the deeper truths in this conflict and approach it with wisdom. Thank you for your gentle insight."

Archangel Sandalphon

On Relationship Conflicts:

Conflict disrupts harmony, but it can also inspire growth. I help you ground yourself, calming the emotional turbulence that often accompanies disagreements. Together, we'll create a steady, balanced approach to resolution, fostering peace and mutual understanding.

Talk to Me:

LIFE THROUGH ANGEL EYES

"Archangel Sandalphon, guide me to stay grounded and approach this conflict with balance and peace. Thank you for your calming presence."

Archangel Jeremiel

On Relationship Conflicts:

Conflict is an opportunity to reflect on your relationships and your role within them. I help you review the dynamics at play, bringing clarity to what needs healing or adjustment. Together, we'll plan for positive change and stronger connections moving forward.

Talk to Me:

"Archangel Jeremiel, guide me to reflect on this conflict and bring clarity and healing to my relationships. Thank you for your loving guidance."

Archangel Raguel

On Relationship Conflicts:

Harmony is possible, even in the midst of conflict. I help restore balance to your relationships by encouraging fairness, understanding, and mutual respect. Together, we'll create a foundation for resolution, ensuring that every voice is heard and valued.

Talk to Me:

"Archangel Raguel, guide me to bring balance and fairness to my relationships, fostering harmony and resolution. Thank you for your supportive wisdom."

Archangel Raziel

CH JODI M DEHN

On Relationship Conflicts:

Conflict often stems from spiritual or emotional disconnection. I help you uncover the hidden wisdom within the disagreement, guiding you to a deeper understanding of yourself and others. Together, we'll align your relationships with divine purpose, creating harmony and growth.

Talk to Me:

"Archangel Raziel, guide me to uncover the deeper spiritual truths within this conflict and align my relationships with divine harmony. Thank you for your enlightening presence."

Archangel Haniel

On Relationship Conflicts:

Conflict disrupts emotional balance, but it also offers a chance to restore harmony. I help you navigate these emotional waves with grace, fostering understanding and calm. Together, we'll embrace the path to resolution, creating relationships filled with peace and balance.

Talk to Me:

"Archangel Haniel, guide me to navigate emotional conflicts with grace and restore harmony in my relationships. Thank you for your calming wisdom."

ON BALANCE

Archangel Michael

On Balance:

Balance begins with establishing clear boundaries, both for yourself and others. I help you identify what aligns with your values and release what no longer serves you. When life feels chaotic, call on me to cut through distractions and guide you back to the center of your strength and integrity.

Talk to Me:

"Archangel Michael, help me set clear boundaries and release distractions so I may restore balance in my life. Thank you for your protective strength."

Archangel Gabriel

On Balance:

Life's balance depends on clear communication—with yourself and others. I guide you to express your needs and desires while listening with compassion. Together, we'll create a rhythm in your life that nurtures joy and creativity while honoring the responsibilities you carry.

Talk to Me:

"Archangel Gabriel, guide me to communicate my needs and find a rhythm that nurtures joy and balance. Thank you for your inspiring guidance."

Archangel Raphael

On Balance:

Balance is essential for physical, emotional, and spiritual health. I bring healing to the areas of your life that feel out of sync, soothing stress and restoring harmony. Together, we'll create habits and routines that support your well-being and align your life with inner peace.

Talk to Me:

"Archangel Raphael, heal the imbalances in my life and guide me to nurture habits that promote peace and well-being. Thank you for your loving care."

Archangel Uriel

On Balance:

True balance comes from inner wisdom and calm. I help you see clearly when life feels overwhelming, illuminating the choices and priorities that will bring peace. Together, we'll find stability and focus, allowing you to handle life's challenges with grace and clarity.

Talk to Me:

"Archangel Uriel, guide me to prioritize wisely and bring calm wisdom to restore balance in my life. Thank you for your enlightening presence."

Archangel Zadkiel

On Balance:

Balance often requires forgiveness—of yourself and others. I help you release guilt, anxiety, and emotional heaviness that weigh you down. Together, we'll replace these burdens with peace, calm, and discernment, allowing your inner world to reflect harmony and balance.

Talk to Me:

"Archangel Zadkiel, help me release emotional burdens and embrace peace so I may restore balance. Thank you for your calming support."

Archangel Metatron

On Balance:

Life's balance often feels elusive, but it begins with organization and clarity. I help you align your goals with your divine purpose, prioritizing what truly matters. Together, we'll bring order to your thoughts and actions, allowing you to create harmony within and around you.

Talk to Me:

"Archangel Metatron, guide me to organize my life and align with my purpose so I may create balance. Thank you for your divine guidance."

Archangel Chamuel

On Balance:

Emotional balance begins with self-love. I guide you to heal feelings of neglect, disconnection, or overextension, helping you honor your needs. Together, we'll nurture your heart and bring peace to your relationships, allowing you to create a life of harmony and inner stability.

Talk to Me:

"Archangel Chamuel, help me honor my emotional needs and create a life filled with love and balance. Thank you for your tender guidance."

Archangel Samuel

On Balance:

Balance requires vitality, and vitality begins with rest and renewal. I help you find the energy to move forward while honoring your need for recuperation. Together, we'll restore your strength and align your actions with a rhythm that sustains both peace and progress.

Talk to Me:

"Archangel Samuel, restore my energy and guide me to honor the rhythm of rest and action in my life. Thank you for your revitalizing support."

Archangel Zachariel

On Balance:

Strength and balance go hand in hand. I help you stand firm in your truth while remaining flexible to life's changes. Together, we'll find the balance between perseverance and adaptability, helping you maintain stability even in the face of challenges.

Talk to Me:

"Archangel Zachariel, help me find strength and adaptability to create balance in my life. Thank you for your unwavering support."

Archangel Jophiel

On Balance:

LIFE THROUGH ANGEL EYES

Balance is found in recognizing the beauty and blessings within your life. I help you shift your focus from stress and chaos to gratitude and harmony. Together, we'll create a perspective that nurtures positivity and restores balance to your thoughts and actions.

Talk to Me:

"Archangel Jophiel, guide me to focus on gratitude and beauty so I may restore balance to my life. Thank you for your uplifting presence."

Archangel Laviah

On Balance:

Balance requires intuition and reflection. I guide you to connect with your inner wisdom, helping you discern what needs attention and what needs release. Together, we'll create harmony between your thoughts, emotions, and actions, aligning you with your highest self.

Talk to Me:

"Archangel Laviah, guide me to trust my intuition and align my actions with inner wisdom. Thank you for your gentle insight."

Archangel Sandalphon

On Balance:

Balance thrives in groundedness and connection. Through prayer, music, or meditation, I help you center yourself, finding harmony between your spiritual and earthly responsibilities. Together, we'll create a sense of peace and rhythm that sustains you through life's demands.

Talk to Me:

"Archangel Sandalphon, help me find groundedness and peace so I may restore balance in my life. Thank you for your steady presence."

Archangel Jeremiel

On Balance:

Balance requires reflection and adjustment. I help you review the patterns in your life, identifying what serves you and what needs change. Together, we'll create a plan for a more harmonious future, bringing your life into alignment with your soul's purpose.

Talk to Me:

"Archangel Jeremiel, guide me to reflect on my life and create a plan for harmony and balance. Thank you for your loving guidance."

Archangel Raguel

On Balance:

Balance in relationships is essential for peace. I help you navigate misunderstandings, ensuring fairness and mutual respect. Together, we'll create harmony in your connections, allowing balance to flourish in all aspects of your relationships and interactions.

Talk to Me:

"Archangel Raguel, guide me to restore harmony and fairness in my relationships so balance may thrive. Thank you for your supportive wisdom."

Archangel Raziel

On Balance:

LIFE THROUGH ANGEL EYES

Balance often requires connecting with the deeper truths of your soul. I help you uncover the spiritual wisdom within you, aligning your actions with your higher self. Together, we'll create a life that reflects harmony between the physical and the spiritual.

Talk to Me:

"Archangel Raziel, guide me to uncover spiritual truths and align my actions with divine balance. Thank you for your enlightening presence."

Archangel Haniel

On Balance:

Balance is the harmony between light and shadow, between emotion and reason. I help you navigate the waves of life with grace, restoring equilibrium when you feel off-center. Together, we'll cultivate a life of peace, stability, and emotional alignment.

Talk to Me:

"Archangel Haniel, guide me to navigate life's waves with grace and restore balance to my heart and mind. Thank you for your calming wisdom."

ON FORGIVENESS

Archangel Michael

On Forgiveness:

Forgiveness is not a weakness—it is your greatest shield. Holding onto anger or pain keeps you tied to the past, but I can help you cut those energetic cords. I will stand with you as you reclaim your strength and release the weight of resentment. Forgiveness clears your path, allowing you to step forward with courage and clarity.

Talk to Me:

"Archangel Michael, help me release the bonds of anger and pain so I can forgive and move forward in strength. Thank you for your protective light."

Archangel Gabriel

On Forgiveness:

Words are powerful, especially those we speak to ourselves. Forgiveness begins with compassion, even when it feels undeserved. I guide you to express the unspoken, whether it's an apology, a reconciliation, or simply a silent acknowledgment of pain. Through these words, we can transform guilt into healing and create space for joy to return.

Talk to Me:

"Archangel Gabriel, guide my words to foster understanding and healing as I work toward forgiveness. Thank you for your gentle inspiration."

LIFE THROUGH ANGEL EYES

Archangel Raphael

On Forgiveness:

Forgiveness is a balm for the soul, a healing force that restores peace to your heart. Emotional wounds can manifest in the body, and by forgiving, you begin to release those stored pains. I will walk with you as you mend the broken places, helping you feel whole and free once more.

Talk to Me:

"Archangel Raphael, soothe the wounds in my heart and body that forgiveness can heal. Thank you for your loving presence."

Archangel Uriel

On Forgiveness:

Clarity is the first step to forgiveness. I shine my light on the confusion and fear that keep you bound to old hurts, helping you see the situation with wisdom. When you understand the lessons hidden within pain, forgiveness comes naturally, opening the door to peace and renewal.

Talk to Me:

"Archangel Uriel, illuminate my heart and mind with wisdom so I can understand and embrace forgiveness. Thank you for your guiding light."

Archangel Zadkiel

On Forgiveness:

Forgiveness transforms pain into peace and regret into wisdom. I help you gently unravel the knots of resentment and fear, showing you how to replace them with calm and compassion. Together, we can dissolve the weight of the past and create space for love and understanding to flourish.

Talk to Me:

"Archangel Zadkiel, help me release resentment and open my heart to the peace that forgiveness brings. Thank you for your compassionate guidance."

Archangel Metatron

On Forgiveness:

Forgiveness is a key to enlightenment. When you forgive, you lighten the burden your soul carries, freeing you to connect with your higher self. I help you see the patterns and lessons in every experience, guiding you to let go with wisdom and embrace your divine journey.

Talk to Me:

"Archangel Metatron, guide me to see the spiritual purpose behind forgiveness and help me release the burdens of my soul. Thank you for your divine clarity."

Archangel Chamuel

On Forgiveness:

Forgiveness begins with the heart. Whether you've been hurt or caused pain, I help you approach yourself and others with unconditional love. Together, we'll heal the inner wounds that block forgiveness, restoring peace and connection to your relationships.

Talk to Me:

LIFE THROUGH ANGEL EYES

"Archangel Chamuel, help me open my heart to forgive myself and others with compassion and love. Thank you for your gentle strength."

Archangel Samuel

On Forgiveness:

Forgiveness revitalizes your spirit, infusing your life with fresh energy and possibility. Whether it's a lingering hurt or a buried grudge, I help you release the heaviness that keeps you stuck. Together, we'll restore vitality to your heart, opening the way for joy and renewal.

Talk to Me:

"Archangel Samuel, infuse my heart with the energy to forgive and embrace the freedom it brings. Thank you for your uplifting presence."

Archangel Zachariel

On Forgiveness:

Forgiveness takes strength, but it's a strength you already possess. I guide you to tap into your inner resilience, empowering you to face the pain and choose healing. Together, we'll transform destructive tendencies like bitterness into the courage to move forward with grace.

Talk to Me:

"Archangel Zachariel, guide me to find the strength within myself to forgive and let go of anger. Thank you for your steadfast support."

Archangel Jophiel

CH JODI M DEHN

On Forgiveness:

Forgiveness brings beauty back to your world. When resentment clouds your vision, I help you see the blessings hidden in even the hardest moments. Together, we'll shift your focus to gratitude and understanding, allowing forgiveness to bloom naturally in your heart.

Talk to Me:

"Archangel Jophiel, help me see the beauty and lessons within my struggles so I may forgive with grace. Thank you for your loving insight."

Archangel Laviah

On Forgiveness:

Forgiveness often begins in dreams and quiet reflections. I guide you to connect with your intuition, revealing the deeper truths behind your pain. In these quiet spaces, we'll uncover the wisdom and peace that make forgiveness possible, even in the most challenging situations.

Talk to Me:

"Archangel Laviah, guide my intuition to uncover the truths that lead to forgiveness and peace. Thank you for your quiet wisdom."

Archangel Sandalphon

On Forgiveness:

Forgiveness is a harmony that resonates deeply within your soul. Through music, prayer, or meditation, I help you connect to the divine rhythm that soothes your heart and releases pain. Together, we'll create a melody of healing that restores balance and grace to your life.

Talk to Me:

"Archangel Sandalphon, help me connect with the divine harmony that fosters forgiveness and peace. Thank you for your grounding presence."

Archangel Jeremiel

On Forgiveness:

Reflecting on the past can be painful, but it's also where forgiveness begins. I help you review your experiences with compassion, guiding you to understand and release the emotions that bind you. Together, we'll create a plan for moving forward, unburdened and renewed.

Talk to Me:

"Archangel Jeremiel, guide me to reflect on my past with compassion so I can release and forgive. Thank you for your gentle encouragement."

Archangel Raguel

On Forgiveness:

Forgiveness restores balance to relationships. When misunderstandings arise, I help you see both sides with fairness and clarity. Together, we'll foster harmony and mutual respect, ensuring forgiveness is rooted in truth and connection rather than obligation.

Talk to Me:

"Archangel Raguel, guide me to find fairness and balance in my relationships so forgiveness can flourish. Thank you for your wise support."

Archangel Raziel

On Forgiveness:

Forgiveness holds deep spiritual wisdom. I help you access the higher truths behind your pain, revealing how even the most difficult experiences can lead to growth. Together, we'll align your soul with divine understanding, allowing forgiveness to unfold naturally and with grace.

Talk to Me:

"Archangel Raziel, guide me to uncover the spiritual lessons behind forgiveness so I may heal and grow. Thank you for your enlightening insight."

Archangel Haniel

On Forgiveness:

Forgiveness is an act of emotional balance. I help you navigate the waves of hurt and disappointment, guiding you to find peace and harmony within. Together, we'll create space for forgiveness to restore your emotional well-being and reconnect you with your inner light.

Talk to Me:

"Archangel Haniel, guide me to find emotional balance and open my heart to forgiveness. Thank you for your calming wisdom."

ON FRIEND CHANGES

Archangel Michael

On Friend Changes:

Friendships shift as your path evolves, but do not fear these changes. I stand by you as relationships end or transform, protecting your heart and helping you see the strength in letting go. Every person serves a purpose on your journey, but not all are meant to walk it forever. Trust that those who leave create space for others to come.

Talk to Me:

"Archangel Michael, guide me through the shifts in my friendships and protect my heart as I let go of what no longer serves me. Thank you for your steadfast presence."

Archangel Gabriel

On Friend Changes:

The seasons of friendships require open communication. I help you express gratitude for those who have been by your side and courage to say goodbye when paths diverge. Changes in friendships aren't failures but opportunities to grow and make room for joy and authenticity in your connections.

Talk to Me:

"Archangel Gabriel, guide my words to honor past friendships and open my heart to new ones. Thank you for inspiring clarity and connection."

Archangel Raphael

On Friend Changes:

Changes in friendships can bring heartache, but I am here to help you heal. As relationships ebb and flow, I will soothe your heart and show you the gift in each connection. Healing comes in honoring the love shared and embracing the wisdom gained, even as paths diverge.

Talk to Me:

"Archangel Raphael, heal the wounds of changing friendships and guide me to see the blessings in their transformations. Thank you for your loving care."

Archangel Uriel

On Friend Changes:

Friendship changes can feel like stepping into the unknown, but clarity is key. I help you find wisdom in these shifts, illuminating the lessons and growth each relationship brings. When friends change or leave, I will show you how their presence shaped your path and prepared you for what's ahead.

Talk to Me:

"Archangel Uriel, guide me to see the wisdom in my friendships as they change and bring clarity to my heart. Thank you for your enlightening presence."

Archangel Zadkiel

On Friend Changes:

Forgiveness often plays a role in friendship changes. Whether you feel hurt or have caused hurt, I guide you to release resentment and find peace in letting go. By cultivating understanding, you allow new friendships to blossom while honoring the beauty of what once was.

Talk to Me:

"Archangel Zadkiel, help me release resentment and find forgiveness in the shifting dynamics of my friendships. Thank you for bringing me peace."

Archangel Metatron

On Friend Changes:

As your purpose evolves, so too will your friendships. I help you align your connections with your higher self, creating space for relationships that resonate with your soul's growth. Some friends are stepping stones, others lifelong companions; both serve divine purposes in your journey.

Talk to Me:

"Archangel Metatron, guide me to align my friendships with my soul's purpose and embrace the evolution of my connections. Thank you for your divine insight."

Archangel Chamuel

On Friend Changes:

When friendships change, it can awaken feelings of abandonment or loss. I guide you to nurture self-love, reminding you that your worth is not tied to the presence of others. By healing your heart, we create space for relationships that reflect the peace and love within you.

Talk to Me:

"Archangel Chamuel, help me nurture self-love and find peace as friendships change. Thank you for guiding me toward relationships that honor my heart."

Archangel Samuel

On Friend Changes:

Transitions in friendships can deplete your energy, leaving you feeling ungrounded. I am here to restore your vitality and help you find balance amid these shifts. Friendships, like all things, ebb and flow, but with renewal comes the possibility of deeper and more fulfilling connections.

Talk to Me:

"Archangel Samuel, restore my energy as I navigate friendship changes and guide me toward renewal and balance. Thank you for your revitalizing presence."

Archangel Zachariel

On Friend Changes:

The strength to accept changes in friendships often feels elusive, but it lies within you. I guide you to face these transitions with resilience and courage, showing you how to embrace the opportunities hidden in endings. Trust that new bonds will arise, stronger and more aligned with your spirit.

Talk to Me:

"Archangel Zachariel, help me find the strength to embrace friendship changes and trust in the relationships to come. Thank you for your steadfast support."

LIFE THROUGH ANGEL EYES

Archangel Jophiel

On Friend Changes:

Friendship changes can feel like losses, but they also create space for gratitude. I help you find beauty in what was shared, shifting your focus from pain to appreciation. Together, we'll honor the joy those connections brought and welcome the promise of new beginnings.

Talk to Me:

"Archangel Jophiel, guide me to see the beauty in past friendships and embrace gratitude for what they brought to my life. Thank you for your uplifting presence."

Archangel Laviah

On Friend Changes:

Dreams and intuition can reveal the deeper truths behind friendship changes. I guide you to reflect on these connections, uncovering their spiritual significance and what your soul needed to learn. In the quiet moments of introspection, we'll find the wisdom to move forward with grace.

Talk to Me:

"Archangel Laviah, help me understand the deeper meaning behind my friendships and navigate their changes with wisdom. Thank you for your quiet guidance."

Archangel Sandalphon

On Friend Changes:

Friendships, like music, have their own rhythm. When the melody shifts, I guide you to find harmony once more. Through prayer or meditation, I help you connect with the divine flow, allowing you to gracefully let go and welcome the new relationships that align with your spirit.

Talk to Me:

"Archangel Sandalphon, help me find harmony in the changing rhythm of my friendships and trust in the divine flow. Thank you for your grounding presence."

Archangel Jeremiel

On Friend Changes:

Reflection is key when friendships evolve. I help you look back with compassion, honoring the lessons and joy each connection brought. Together, we'll create a vision for the future, inviting relationships that align with your growth and bring even greater fulfillment.

Talk to Me:

"Archangel Jeremiel, guide me to reflect on my friendships with compassion and embrace the changes that lead to greater connection. Thank you for your loving insight."

Archangel Raguel

On Friend Changes:

When friendships change due to misunderstandings or conflict, I bring fairness and harmony to the situation. Whether reconciliation or release is needed, I help you navigate the path with balance and mutual respect, restoring peace to your heart and relationships.

Talk to Me:

LIFE THROUGH ANGEL EYES

"Archangel Raguel, guide me to find fairness and harmony in my friendships as they evolve. Thank you for your balanced wisdom."

Archangel Raziel

On Friend Changes:

Friendship changes are often part of a greater spiritual journey. I help you see the divine plan behind these shifts, connecting you with the wisdom and growth each relationship offers. Together, we'll align your connections with the greater purpose of your soul.

Talk to Me:

"Archangel Raziel, guide me to see the divine purpose behind the changes in my friendships and embrace the growth they bring. Thank you for your illuminating guidance."

Archangel Haniel

On Friend Changes:

Changes in friendships can stir deep emotions, but balance is key. I help you navigate the waves of grief, relief, or uncertainty, restoring harmony to your heart. Together, we'll create space for new connections while honoring the emotional truth of what you're leaving behind.

Talk to Me:

"Archangel Haniel, help me find emotional balance as I navigate the changes in my friendships. Thank you for your steady, calming presence."

ON BULLYING

Archangel Michael

On Bullying:

I am your protector, standing as a shield between you and those who seek to harm you. Bullying tries to rob you of your courage, but I remind you of your power. Together, we'll cut the cords of fear and doubt, empowering you to face these challenges with strength. You are not alone, and I will guard your heart through every storm.

Talk to Me:

"Archangel Michael, protect me from harm and give me the courage to stand tall in the face of bullying. Thank you for your unwavering strength."

Archangel Gabriel

On Bullying:

Words can wound deeply, but they can also heal. I help you find your voice, empowering you to express yourself with confidence and clarity. Whether you need to speak out, seek support, or simply remind yourself of your worth, I guide you to use the power of communication to restore your joy and self-belief.

Talk to Me:

"Archangel Gabriel, guide my words and help me find the courage to speak up for myself with clarity and strength. Thank you for your inspiration."

Archangel Raphael

LIFE THROUGH ANGEL EYES

On Bullying:

Bullying leaves scars, both seen and unseen. I am here to heal those wounds. With my light, I soothe the pain of unkindness and help you reclaim the wholeness that bullying tries to take from you. Together, we'll restore your confidence and show you the beauty of your resilient spirit.

Talk to Me:

"Archangel Raphael, heal the wounds caused by bullying and help me rediscover my strength and self-worth. Thank you for your tender care."

Archangel Uriel

On Bullying:

Bullying thrives on confusion and fear, but I bring clarity and peace. I help you see the situation from a higher perspective, revealing the insecurities behind the actions of others. With this understanding, we can transform your fear into wisdom and guide you toward solutions that empower you.

Talk to Me:

"Archangel Uriel, shine your light of wisdom on my situation and guide me to find peace and strength amid bullying. Thank you for your clarity."

Archangel Zadkiel

On Bullying:

When bullying triggers anxiety or self-doubt, I help you find calm within the chaos. Together, we'll transform feelings of helplessness into self-compassion and strength. I guide you toward forgiveness—not to excuse harm but to release its grip on your heart. Peace begins when you let go.

Talk to Me:

"Archangel Zadkiel, help me find calm and release the pain caused by bullying. Guide me toward forgiveness and inner peace. Thank you for your loving presence."

Archangel Metatron

On Bullying:

Bullying often targets the light within you, but your divine spark cannot be diminished. I help you connect with your higher self, reminding you of your true worth and purpose. Together, we'll rise above the negativity, creating a space where your light can shine freely.

Talk to Me:

"Archangel Metatron, help me rise above the negativity of bullying and reconnect with my divine purpose. Thank you for your wisdom and guidance."

Archangel Chamuel

On Bullying:

Bullying can make you feel abandoned and unworthy, but I am here to guide you back to love—especially self-love. I help you heal the wounds inflicted by cruelty and strengthen your connection to your inner child. Together, we'll nurture your heart and remind you that you are deeply loved.

LIFE THROUGH ANGEL EYES

Talk to Me:

"Archangel Chamuel, help me heal the pain of bullying and restore my self-love and confidence. Thank you for your compassionate guidance."

Archangel Samuel

On Bullying:

The weight of bullying can drain your energy and leave you feeling defeated. I am here to renew your vitality and help you find balance once more. Together, we'll restore your spirit, replacing fear and despair with the strength and hope needed to move forward.

Talk to Me:

"Archangel Samuel, replenish my energy and help me find balance and hope in the face of bullying. Thank you for your revitalizing presence."

Archangel Zachariel

On Bullying:

Strength is the answer to bullying—not physical strength but the quiet, unshakable kind within you. I guide you to discover your inner resilience, helping you stand tall no matter how others try to bring you down. Together, we'll transform pain into power and fear into courage.

Talk to Me:

"Archangel Zachariel, help me tap into my inner strength and face bullying with resilience and courage. Thank you for your unwavering support."

CH JODI M DEHN

Archangel Jophiel

On Bullying:

Bullying distorts how you see yourself, but I am here to show you the truth of your beauty and worth. I help you shift your focus from the unkindness of others to the goodness within you. Together, we'll fill your heart with gratitude for the light you carry.

Talk to Me:

"Archangel Jophiel, help me see the beauty and worth within myself, even when others try to diminish it. Thank you for your uplifting guidance."

Archangel Laviah

On Bullying:

In the quiet of your dreams or moments of stillness, I help you process the emotions and pain bullying creates. I guide your intuition to reveal the truths you need, whether it's the courage to seek help or the wisdom to let go. Together, we'll uncover a path to healing.

Talk to Me:

"Archangel Laviah, guide my intuition to help me process and heal from the pain of bullying. Thank you for your quiet wisdom."

Archangel Sandalphon

On Bullying:

The aggression of bullying can leave you feeling ungrounded and adrift. I help you reconnect with the earth's calming energy and the divine harmony of music or prayer. Together, we'll replace discord

LIFE THROUGH ANGEL EYES

with balance, grounding you in your strength and helping you find peace amid chaos.

Talk to Me:

"Archangel Sandalphon, help me find harmony and groundedness amid the chaos of bullying. Thank you for your calming presence."

Archangel Jeremiel

On Bullying:

Bullying can cloud your emotions, but I help you reflect with clarity and compassion. Together, we'll identify the lessons within the experience and create a plan to move forward, free from the pain others have caused. Every ending leads to a new beginning filled with hope.

Talk to Me:

"Archangel Jeremiel, guide me to reflect on my experiences with bullying and move forward with hope and clarity. Thank you for your encouraging presence."

Archangel Raguel

On Bullying:

Bullying often thrives on misunderstandings and imbalance, but I restore fairness and harmony. I help you navigate the dynamics of these relationships with wisdom, showing you how to stand up for yourself while maintaining your inner peace. Justice, fairness, and resolution are within reach.

Talk to Me:

"Archangel Raguel, bring balance and fairness to my relationships and help me navigate bullying with wisdom. Thank you for your steady guidance."

Archangel Raziel

On Bullying:

Bullying can feel overwhelming, but it's part of a larger spiritual journey. I help you uncover the lessons and truths hidden within these challenges, connecting you with your divine power. Together, we'll transform this pain into wisdom that strengthens your spirit and aligns you with your higher self.

Talk to Me:

"Archangel Raziel, reveal the spiritual lessons behind my experiences with bullying and guide me toward growth and understanding. Thank you for your illuminating support."

Archangel Haniel

On Bullying:

The emotional waves of bullying can feel relentless, but I help you find balance within. Together, we'll calm the storms of anger, sadness, or fear, restoring harmony to your heart. Forgiveness—for yourself and others—will become the anchor that keeps you steady.

Talk to Me:

"Archangel Haniel, help me find emotional balance and forgive myself and others amid the challenges of bullying. Thank you for your soothing presence."

ON GOAL SETTING

Archangel Michael

On Goal Setting:

Goals require strength, determination, and clear boundaries. I help you stay focused by cutting away distractions and doubts. Fear of failure will not deter you while I stand by your side. Together, we'll fortify your resolve, ensuring that each step you take is purposeful and aligned with your ultimate vision.

Talk to Me:

"Archangel Michael, shield me from distractions and doubts as I set and pursue my goals. Thank you for your steadfast support and encouragement."

Archangel Gabriel

On Goal Setting:

Your goals need clear expression to take root in reality. I assist you in articulating your dreams, writing them down, or sharing them with others. Creativity and joy will flow as you take your first steps. Trust your voice, and let your ambitions sing loud and true.

Talk to Me:

"Archangel Gabriel, inspire me to articulate my goals with clarity and bring creativity to my efforts. Thank you for guiding me toward fulfillment."

Archangel Raphael

On Goal Setting:

Your goals must nourish your soul and body. I guide you to choose paths that promote balance, healing, and wellness. If your ambitions feel overwhelming or stressful, I help you refocus on what truly matters, ensuring that your journey is one of growth and renewal.

Talk to Me:

"Archangel Raphael, guide me to set goals that honor my well-being and help me maintain balance as I work toward them. Thank you for your healing wisdom."

Archangel Uriel

On Goal Setting:

Every goal begins with wisdom and inspiration. I illuminate your path, helping you see the bigger picture and prioritize what aligns with your soul's growth. When uncertainty clouds your vision, I will shine a light on the steps ahead, ensuring that each choice is guided by divine insight.

Talk to Me:

"Archangel Uriel, enlighten my path as I set my goals, and help me make wise choices that align with my higher purpose. Thank you for your clarity."

Archangel Zadkiel

On Goal Setting:

Discernment is key in setting meaningful goals. I help you identify what truly resonates with your spirit and release ambitions driven by fear, ego, or societal pressure. Together, we'll create a vision that nurtures your growth, cultivating forgiveness for past missteps and wisdom for future plans.

LIFE THROUGH ANGEL EYES

Talk to Me:

"Archangel Zadkiel, guide me to set goals with discernment and help me release old patterns that no longer serve me. Thank you for your compassionate guidance."

Archangel Metatron

On Goal Setting:

Goal setting is a sacred act of aligning with your soul's purpose. I help you access the divine blueprint of your life, organizing your thoughts and plans into manageable steps. With me, you'll not only dream but also structure those dreams into achievable milestones.

Talk to Me:

"Archangel Metatron, help me align my goals with my higher purpose and organize my path forward with clarity. Thank you for your divine insight."

Archangel Chamuel

On Goal Setting:

Goals grounded in self-love and peace will blossom. I guide you to nurture your inner child, ensuring that your ambitions come from a place of wholeness rather than fear or comparison. Together, we'll create goals that bring harmony to your heart and joy to your journey.

Talk to Me:

"Archangel Chamuel, guide me to set goals that honor my self-love and bring peace to my heart. Thank you for your gentle encouragement."

CH JODI M DEHN

Archangel Samuel

On Goal Setting:

Vitality and focus are essential to reaching your goals. I energize your spirit, helping you overcome fatigue and stay committed. When doubts creep in or you feel stuck, I renew your strength and passion, ensuring that you have the stamina to see your dreams through.

Talk to Me:

"Archangel Samuel, renew my energy and passion as I pursue my goals. Thank you for your invigorating support."

Archangel Zachariel

On Goal Setting:

I am here to help you find the inner strength to tackle challenges on your path to success. Goals may require resilience, and I will fortify you against setbacks. Together, we'll turn obstacles into stepping stones, helping you build a future founded on perseverance and determination.

Talk to Me:

"Archangel Zachariel, help me build the strength and resilience I need to achieve my goals. Thank you for your steady encouragement."

Archangel Jophiel

On Goal Setting:

Goals are more than tasks; they are opportunities to create beauty in your life. I help you see the joy and gratitude in the process, even when progress is slow. Together, we'll focus on the positive and embrace the lessons each step brings, turning every moment into a masterpiece.

Talk to Me:

"Archangel Jophiel, help me see the beauty in my journey toward my goals and keep my focus on the positive. Thank you for your uplifting guidance."

Archangel Laviah

On Goal Setting:

In the quiet of dreams and intuition, your true goals emerge. I guide you to listen to your inner wisdom, uncovering ambitions that align with your soul's desires. Trust the revelations that come in moments of stillness; they hold the keys to your most authentic path forward.

Talk to Me:

"Archangel Laviah, guide my intuition to reveal the goals that align with my soul's purpose. Thank you for your quiet inspiration."

Archangel Sandalphon

On Goal Setting:

Goals, like music, have their own rhythm. I help you stay grounded while attuning to the divine flow of your ambitions. Through prayer, meditation, or song, we'll harmonize your energy with your intentions, creating a steady cadence that leads you toward success.

Talk to Me:

"Archangel Sandalphon, help me stay grounded and aligned with the divine rhythm of my goals. Thank you for your steady guidance."

Archangel Jeremiel

On Goal Setting:

Reflection is vital before setting goals. I help you review where you've been, what you've learned, and what you truly desire. Together, we'll create a plan that honors your past while paving the way for positive change and a bright future filled with hope.

Talk to Me:

"Archangel Jeremiel, guide me in reflecting on my past to create meaningful goals for the future. Thank you for your loving insight."

Archangel Raguel

On Goal Setting:

Relationships can either hinder or support your goals. I bring harmony to your connections, ensuring that your environment nurtures your ambitions. If conflict arises, I guide you to restore balance so you can focus on achieving what matters most without unnecessary distractions.

Talk to Me:

"Archangel Raguel, help me create harmonious relationships that support my goals and remove any conflicts holding me back. Thank you for your wise assistance."

Archangel Raziel

On Goal Setting:

The deepest goals often come from a place of divine inspiration. I help you connect with the mysteries of your soul, unlocking the knowledge and purpose hidden within. Together, we'll align your ambitions with the sacred truths of your being, ensuring your journey is spiritually fulfilling.

Talk to Me:

"Archangel Raziel, help me uncover the divine purpose behind my goals and align my efforts with spiritual truth. Thank you for your enlightening guidance."

Archangel Haniel

On Goal Setting:

Setting goals requires harmony between ambition and patience. I guide you to balance your emotions and energy, ensuring that your goals are realistic yet inspiring. Together, we'll cultivate the grace to work steadily without becoming overwhelmed, trusting in divine timing for your success.

Talk to Me:

"Archangel Haniel, help me find balance as I pursue my goals, and remind me to trust in divine timing. Thank you for your calming presence."

ON SLEEP

Archangel Michael

On Sleep:

Sleep is your sanctuary, a time to rest your body and shield your soul. I stand guard over you as you drift into the quiet realms of dreams. Whatever fears or anxieties keep you awake, release them to me. My protection creates a safe space for peaceful rest, free of worry.

Talk to Me:

"Archangel Michael, stand guard over me as I sleep and protect me from any fears or anxieties that disturb my rest. Thank you for your strength and watchfulness."

Archangel Gabriel

On Sleep:

Sleep is a gateway to divine communication, a time when the veil is thin, and inspiration flows. I help bring clarity to your dreams, offering messages of hope, guidance, and creativity. Trust the visions that come to you in sleep—they are gifts from the divine, meant to guide your waking life.

Talk to Me:

"Archangel Gabriel, bring me messages of clarity and inspiration in my dreams. Help me awaken refreshed and ready to act on your guidance. Thank you for your light."

Archangel Raphael

On Sleep:

LIFE THROUGH ANGEL EYES

Sleep is a powerful tool for healing. As you rest, your body renews itself, and your spirit finds balance. I surround you with my emerald light, soothing your mind and relaxing your body so you can slip into deep, restorative slumber. Healing comes naturally when you allow yourself to truly rest.

Talk to Me:

"Archangel Raphael, guide me into restful sleep and surround me with healing energy as I renew my mind, body, and spirit. Thank you for your soothing care."

Archangel Uriel

On Sleep:

Sleep is a time for illumination and release. I help you let go of the worries and burdens of the day, replacing them with divine wisdom and tranquility. If your mind races or fears keep you awake, call on me. I will bring clarity and peace to your restless thoughts.

Talk to Me:

"Archangel Uriel, calm my restless mind and replace my worries with divine wisdom and peace as I sleep. Thank you for your steady light."

Archangel Zadkiel

On Sleep:

Sleep is your reset button, an opportunity to cleanse your spirit of the day's negativity. I help you release stress, guilt, and self-judgment so you can find the calm and comfort you need for deep rest. Let your dreams be filled with forgiveness, understanding, and gentle renewal.

Talk to Me:

"Archangel Zadkiel, help me release negativity and self-doubt as I sleep. Fill my dreams with peace and renewal. Thank you for your compassionate guidance."

Archangel Metatron

On Sleep:

Sleep aligns your soul with the higher dimensions. I help you organize your thoughts and experiences so that your spirit can ascend in the dream world. If you feel restless or overwhelmed, call on me to clear your mind and bring balance, allowing sleep to become a sacred time of alignment.

Talk to Me:

"Archangel Metatron, guide me into restful sleep and align my spirit with divine purpose as I dream. Thank you for your divine insight and clarity."

Archangel Chamuel

On Sleep:

Sleep is a time to reconnect with your inner peace and self-love. I nurture your heart, quieting the turmoil of the day so you can rest deeply. If you feel lonely or unsettled, let my love envelop you, reminding you that you are cherished and safe.

Talk to Me:

"Archangel Chamuel, bring me peace and comfort as I sleep, reminding me of my worth and helping me awaken renewed in self-love. Thank you for your tenderness."

LIFE THROUGH ANGEL EYES

Archangel Samuel

On Sleep:

Sleep restores your vitality and prepares you for the challenges ahead. I help you find balance between the day's demands and the rest you need. If sleep has become elusive, I calm your body and mind, ensuring that you wake refreshed and ready to embrace life with energy.

Talk to Me:

"Archangel Samuel, calm my mind and body to help me find deep, restorative sleep. Renew my energy for the day ahead. Thank you for your revitalizing presence."

Archangel Zachariel

On Sleep:

Strength often begins with rest. I help you find the resilience to let go of your worries as you sleep, fortifying your spirit for the day to come. Together, we'll turn sleepless nights into moments of quiet strength, where your soul can recharge and face challenges with new vigor.

Talk to Me:

"Archangel Zachariel, help me find the strength to release my worries and sleep peacefully. Renew my spirit as I rest. Thank you for your unwavering support."

Archangel Jophiel

On Sleep:

Even in sleep, beauty surrounds you. I guide you to focus on positive, peaceful thoughts as you drift off, filling your dreams with gratitude and light. Let your sleep become a time of creative inspiration and quiet appreciation, preparing you to wake with joy and clarity.

Talk to Me:

"Archangel Jophiel, fill my dreams with beauty and light, helping me sleep peacefully and wake with joy. Thank you for your uplifting guidance."

Archangel Laviah

On Sleep:

Dreams are my domain, where mysteries unfold and intuition deepens. I guide you into the realm of rest, where revelations and insights emerge. Trust the wisdom of your dreams—they are gifts meant to guide your waking life. Surrender to sleep, and let your intuition blossom.

Talk to Me:

"Archangel Laviah, guide me into dreams filled with wisdom and revelations. Help me awaken with clarity and peace. Thank you for your quiet guidance."

Archangel Sandalphon

On Sleep:

Sleep is a time for harmony and grounding. Through the vibrations of music or prayer, I help you release tension and enter a state of calm. If your mind feels chaotic, let divine melodies soothe you, creating the balance you need to rest deeply.

Talk to Me:

"Archangel Sandalphon, bring harmony and peace to my mind and guide me into restful sleep. Thank you for your grounding presence."

Archangel Jeremiel

On Sleep:

Sleep is a time for reflection, a chance to process the day's emotions and plan for positive change. I help you review your experiences with clarity and compassion, easing your mind into peaceful rest. Tomorrow is a new beginning, and I will help you prepare for it with hope.

Talk to Me:

"Archangel Jeremiel, help me process the emotions of the day and guide me toward peaceful sleep and a hopeful tomorrow. Thank you for your gentle encouragement."

Archangel Raguel

On Sleep:

Balance in relationships and emotions often determines the quality of your rest. I help you resolve inner conflicts and restore harmony to your heart, ensuring that you drift into sleep free of tension. Trust that peace can replace discord, even as you rest.

Talk to Me:

"Archangel Raguel, restore balance and harmony in my emotions and relationships so I can sleep peacefully. Thank you for your steady guidance."

Archangel Raziel

CH JODI M DEHN

On Sleep:

In sleep, the secrets of the universe whisper to your soul. I help you access the hidden knowledge and spiritual truths that come through dreams. Trust that each night is an opportunity to connect with the divine and awaken with wisdom to guide your journey.

Talk to Me:

"Archangel Raziel, guide me to uncover spiritual truths in my dreams and help me awaken with clarity and purpose. Thank you for your enlightening presence."

Archangel Haniel

On Sleep:

Sleep is a delicate balance between surrender and renewal. I help you find harmony within yourself so that rest can come easily. When frustration or restlessness disturbs your nights, I soothe your emotions and align your energy with the calming rhythms of the universe. Sleep becomes not just rest but a restoration of inner balance and grace.

Talk to Me:

"Archangel Haniel, bring balance to my mind and emotions so I can surrender to peaceful sleep. Restore my spirit with harmony and grace. Thank you for your calming light."

ON LIFE PURPOSE

Archangel Michael

On Life Purpose:

Your purpose is your strength. I am here to help you cut through doubts and fears that obscure your path. Life purpose is not always clear, but with my sword of light, I will help you reveal the truth within yourself. Stand firm, and I will guide you to courageously embrace your mission.

Talk to Me:

"Archangel Michael, clear away my doubts and fears as I search for my life purpose. Help me stand strong and follow the path meant for me. Thank you for your unwavering strength."

Archangel Gabriel

On Life Purpose:

Your life purpose often whispers to you through creativity, joy, and expression. I help you listen to that inner voice and communicate your dreams to the world. When you feel lost, trust me to inspire you with divine clarity and help you align your purpose with your unique gifts.

Talk to Me:

"Archangel Gabriel, inspire me with clarity and confidence to align my life purpose with my gifts. Thank you for guiding me to express my truest self."

Archangel Raphael

CH JODI M DEHN

On Life Purpose:

Your life purpose is intimately connected to your well-being. I help you see the connections between what heals your body, soothes your spirit, and fulfills your soul. Together, we will find a path that promotes not only your growth but also your ability to heal and uplift others.

Talk to Me:

"Archangel Raphael, guide me toward a life purpose that aligns with healing and wholeness for myself and others. Thank you for your loving guidance."

Archangel Uriel

On Life Purpose:

Your purpose shines brightest when illuminated by wisdom. I am here to help you understand the lessons of your life and use them to shape a meaningful future. When despair clouds your way, I'll bring peace and insight, helping you see how every experience contributes to your divine path.

Talk to Me:

"Archangel Uriel, bring your light of wisdom to help me understand my life purpose and guide me forward with clarity and peace. Thank you for your illuminating presence."

Archangel Zadkiel

On Life Purpose:

Discovering your life purpose requires forgiveness—for others and for yourself. I help you release the burdens of guilt and regret,

LIFE THROUGH ANGEL EYES

clearing space for discernment and wisdom. Your path is sacred, and together we will create a vision of purpose that reflects your highest potential and divine love.

Talk to Me:

"Archangel Zadkiel, help me release the past and embrace discernment as I uncover my life purpose. Thank you for your wisdom and compassion."

Archangel Metatron

On Life Purpose:

Your purpose is written in the divine blueprint of your soul. I help you access the records of your existence, showing you how every choice and experience aligns with your higher calling. Together, we'll bring structure to your spiritual journey, allowing you to fulfill your destiny with clarity and confidence.

Talk to Me:

"Archangel Metatron, reveal the divine blueprint of my soul and guide me to fulfill my life purpose with clarity. Thank you for your sacred guidance."

Archangel Chamuel

On Life Purpose:

Your life purpose begins with self-love. I guide you to reconnect with your heart, nurturing your inner child and healing wounds that block your path. When you love yourself fully, your purpose unfolds naturally, creating harmony in your relationships and the world around you.

Talk to Me:

"Archangel Chamuel, guide me to love myself fully so I can embrace and fulfill my life purpose. Thank you for your gentle and healing presence."

Archangel Samuel

On Life Purpose:

Vitality is key to discovering your life purpose. I help you tap into your energy and passion, removing the stagnation that keeps you stuck. Your mission is alive within you, waiting for renewal. Let me invigorate your spirit so you can step forward with confidence and strength.

Talk to Me:

"Archangel Samuel, renew my energy and passion to help me uncover and pursue my life purpose. Thank you for your empowering guidance."

Archangel Zachariel

On Life Purpose:

Your purpose often requires strength and perseverance. I help you confront challenges that may block your path and transform them into stepping stones. Even in moments of doubt or destruction, I am here to remind you that you are capable of rebuilding a meaningful life aligned with your divine mission.

Talk to Me:

"Archangel Zachariel, give me the strength to overcome challenges as I uncover my life purpose. Thank you for your steadfast support."

LIFE THROUGH ANGEL EYES

Archangel Jophiel

On Life Purpose:

Your life purpose is deeply tied to the beauty of your spirit. I help you find gratitude and joy in the small moments, teaching you to see how they contribute to the larger masterpiece of your existence. With positivity and understanding, your purpose will become as clear as sunlight.

Talk to Me:

"Archangel Jophiel, bring clarity and joy to my search for my life purpose. Help me see the beauty in every step of my journey. Thank you for your radiant guidance."

Archangel Laviah

On Life Purpose:

Your purpose is often revealed in dreams and quiet moments of intuition. I guide you to listen to your inner wisdom, helping you connect with the divine messages that are woven into your subconscious. Trust your instincts—they are the compass pointing toward your true calling.

Talk to Me:

"Archangel Laviah, guide me to listen to my inner wisdom and dreams as I discover my life purpose. Thank you for your subtle and profound insights."

Archangel Sandalphon

On Life Purpose:

Your life purpose carries its own rhythm, much like music. I help you tune into the divine harmony of your life, grounding you in faith and balance. When chaos disrupts your sense of direction, let me guide you back to the steady beat of your soul's unique melody.

Talk to Me:

"Archangel Sandalphon, help me find the divine rhythm of my life purpose and guide me toward balance and fulfillment. Thank you for your grounding presence."

Archangel Jeremiel

On Life Purpose:

Reflection is the key to understanding your purpose. I help you review your life with compassion, showing you how every moment—both joyful and painful—has prepared you for your path. Together, we will create a vision for the future that honors your experiences and aligns with your soul's mission.

Talk to Me:

"Archangel Jeremiel, guide me in reflecting on my life to uncover my purpose and align with my highest good. Thank you for your wisdom and love."

Archangel Raguel

On Life Purpose:

Harmonious relationships often reveal your life purpose. I help you restore balance in your connections, showing you how to learn from others while staying true to yourself. When conflicts arise, I bring clarity and peace, ensuring that your journey is supported by understanding and love.

LIFE THROUGH ANGEL EYES

Talk to Me:

"Archangel Raguel, guide me to find harmony in my relationships as I uncover my life purpose. Thank you for your steady and nurturing guidance."

Archangel Raziel

On Life Purpose:

Your life purpose is encoded in the mysteries of the universe. I help you uncover the spiritual truths and divine knowledge hidden within your soul. Together, we will explore the sacred wisdom of your being, aligning your purpose with the eternal flow of creation.

Talk to Me:

"Archangel Raziel, reveal the divine mysteries that align with my life purpose and guide me toward spiritual fulfillment. Thank you for your sacred insights."

Archangel Haniel

On Life Purpose:

Your life purpose is a delicate balance between aspiration and grace. I guide you to find harmony in your ambitions, ensuring that your journey is both meaningful and fulfilling. Trust that your purpose is not a destination but a dance between intention and divine timing.

Talk to Me:

"Archangel Haniel, help me find balance and harmony as I seek my life purpose. Thank you for your calming and gentle presence."

ON NEW RELATIONSHIPS

Archangel Michael

On New Relationships:

New relationships call for courage and clear boundaries. I will help you cut through doubts and fears, guiding you to build a foundation of trust and respect. As protector, I ensure your heart stays safe while allowing it to open fully. Be bold; love requires strength.

Talk to Me:

"Archangel Michael, guide me in building a strong, respectful foundation for this new relationship. Help me embrace love with courage and clarity. Thank you for your unwavering protection."

Archangel Gabriel

On New Relationships:

Communication is the lifeblood of any new bond. I help you speak from your heart, express your feelings authentically, and truly listen. A new relationship thrives when joy and honesty flow freely. Let me nurture this connection with divine clarity and inspiration.

Talk to Me:

"Archangel Gabriel, help me communicate openly and joyfully in this new relationship. Bless our bond with clarity and mutual understanding. Thank you for your loving guidance."

Archangel Raphael

On New Relationships:

LIFE THROUGH ANGEL EYES

Every new relationship offers the chance for healing. I guide you to release old wounds and step into this connection with a fresh, open heart. Together, we'll create a space for love that nurtures and restores your spirit, allowing both of you to grow in harmony.

Talk to Me:

"Archangel Raphael, heal my heart and guide me to nurture this new relationship with love and care. Thank you for your gentle wisdom."

Archangel Uriel

On New Relationships:

A new relationship is a time to embrace wisdom and peace. I help you let go of fears and insecurities, allowing divine clarity to illuminate your path. Trust that this connection is part of your greater journey, and let me guide you toward understanding and serenity.

Talk to Me:

"Archangel Uriel, bring peace and wisdom to my heart as I navigate this new relationship. Help me see its divine purpose. Thank you for your steady light."

Archangel Zadkiel

On New Relationships:

Patience and forgiveness are vital in any budding connection. I help you release past hurts and approach this new bond with an open, discerning heart. Together, we will build a foundation of mutual respect and understanding, free of the burdens of the past.

Talk to Me:

"Archangel Zadkiel, help me approach this new relationship with forgiveness and discernment. Guide us to build a bond rooted in love and respect. Thank you for your calm wisdom."

Archangel Metatron

On New Relationships:

New relationships are opportunities to align your life with higher purpose. I help you organize the chaos of emotions and intentions, bringing balance to this connection. Together, we will create a partnership that resonates with divine harmony and spiritual growth.

Talk to Me:

"Archangel Metatron, guide me to align this new relationship with divine purpose. Help me find balance and clarity in our connection. Thank you for your sacred guidance."

Archangel Chamuel

On New Relationships:

Every new relationship begins with love—for yourself and for another. I guide you to cultivate self-worth so you can approach this bond with an open, confident heart. Let me help you foster peace, trust, and emotional healing as you build this new connection.

Talk to Me:

"Archangel Chamuel, guide me to approach this new relationship with self-love and confidence. Help us create a bond filled with peace and trust. Thank you for your gentle care."

Archangel Samuel

LIFE THROUGH ANGEL EYES

On New Relationships:

A new relationship can bring vitality to your life. I help you embrace the energy and passion this connection offers while ensuring you maintain balance. Together, we'll cultivate a bond that renews your spirit and strengthens your commitment to growth.

Talk to Me:

"Archangel Samuel, guide me to embrace the passion and renewal of this new relationship while maintaining balance. Thank you for your steady presence."

Archangel Zachariel

On New Relationships:

Every new bond requires strength and resolve. I help you navigate challenges and doubts that arise, fortifying your spirit to overcome obstacles. Together, we'll build a relationship that reflects resilience, trust, and the courage to love deeply.

Talk to Me:

"Archangel Zachariel, give me strength and resilience as I navigate this new relationship. Help us overcome challenges with trust and love. Thank you for your support."

Archangel Jophiel

On New Relationships:

A new relationship is a time to see beauty in yourself and the other person. I guide you to appreciate the joy and wonder of this fresh connection, helping you focus on positivity and gratitude. Together, we'll make your bond a source of light and inspiration.

Talk to Me:

"Archangel Jophiel, help me see the beauty in this new relationship and approach it with gratitude and positivity. Thank you for your uplifting guidance."

Archangel Laviah

On New Relationships:

A new relationship is an intuitive journey. I guide you to trust your instincts and listen to the deeper truths of your soul. Dreams and quiet moments often hold the answers you seek about this connection. Trust in the wisdom of your heart.

Talk to Me:

"Archangel Laviah, guide me to trust my intuition and recognize the deeper truths in this new relationship. Thank you for your quiet wisdom."

Archangel Sandalphon

On New Relationships:

New relationships thrive on harmony and balance. I guide you to stay grounded while exploring the emotional highs of this connection. Through music or prayer, I help you find the rhythm of your bond, ensuring it flows with divine grace.

Talk to Me:

"Archangel Sandalphon, help me create harmony and balance in this new relationship. Guide us to find a rhythm that reflects divine grace. Thank you for your grounding presence."

Archangel Jeremiel

LIFE THROUGH ANGEL EYES

On New Relationships:

A new relationship is a time for reflection and hope. I help you understand past patterns and use those lessons to build a brighter future. Let me guide you to create a connection filled with clarity, forgiveness, and the promise of positive change.

Talk to Me:

"Archangel Jeremiel, guide me to reflect on my past and build this new relationship with clarity and hope. Thank you for your loving encouragement."

Archangel Raguel

On New Relationships:

Harmony is the cornerstone of any new connection. I help you create balance and mutual understanding, ensuring your relationship thrives on fairness and respect. When conflicts arise, I bring peace, helping you resolve them with grace and love.

Talk to Me:

"Archangel Raguel, guide me to create harmony and mutual understanding in this new relationship. Help us resolve challenges with grace. Thank you for your steady guidance."

Archangel Raziel

On New Relationships:

New relationships are sacred journeys of discovery. I help you tap into divine mysteries and understand the deeper purpose of your connection. Together, we'll explore the spiritual lessons this bond offers, aligning your love with universal truth and wisdom.

CH JODI M DEHN

Talk to Me:

"Archangel Raziel, reveal the spiritual truths and lessons within this new relationship. Help me align our bond with divine purpose. Thank you for your sacred insight."

Archangel Haniel

On New Relationships:

A new relationship is a dance of balance and grace. I help you stay centered while embracing the excitement of this fresh connection. Together, we'll create harmony between your emotions and intentions, allowing love to flourish with elegance and ease.

Talk to Me:

"Archangel Haniel, guide me to create balance and grace in this new relationship. Help me approach it with emotional harmony and clarity. Thank you for your gentle guidance."

ON EXPECTATIONS

Archangel Michael

On Expectations:

Expectations are powerful, but they can also bind you in fear. I am here to teach you to set expectations with courage and clarity. Release the fear of failure, and trust in your ability to rise to the occasion. Expectations should inspire you, not weigh you down.

Talk to Me:

"Archangel Michael, help me release the fears that come with expectations. Guide me to set them with strength and clarity. Thank you for your unwavering protection."

Archangel Gabriel

On Expectations:

Expectations thrive when communicated clearly and with love. I guide you to express your hopes and listen to others' needs with an open heart. True understanding is born when expectations are shared with kindness, leaving no room for resentment or confusion.

Talk to Me:

"Archangel Gabriel, help me communicate my expectations clearly and lovingly. Guide me to create understanding and harmony in all my relationships. Thank you for your guidance."

Archangel Raphael

On Expectations:

Sometimes, expectations can create tension in your spirit and body. I am here to soothe the weight of unmet hopes and help you align your desires with peace and healing. When you approach life with balance, expectations become gentle markers, not burdens.

Talk to Me:

"Archangel Raphael, help me release the stress of expectations and guide me to align my desires with peace and healing. Thank you for your soothing light."

Archangel Uriel

On Expectations:

Expectations can cloud your mind if not rooted in wisdom. I help you discern realistic goals from those born of fear or desperation. Trust my light to illuminate the path toward meaningful expectations that align with your higher purpose.

Talk to Me:

"Archangel Uriel, guide me to set expectations that align with wisdom and purpose. Help me discern what truly serves my soul. Thank you for your steady light."

Archangel Zadkiel

On Expectations:

Unmet expectations can lead to pain, but forgiveness unlocks freedom. I help you release disappointments and replace them with discernment. With my guidance, you will learn to hold expectations lightly, allowing life to surprise you with its divine grace.

Talk to Me:

LIFE THROUGH ANGEL EYES

"Archangel Zadkiel, help me forgive unmet expectations and teach me to hold space for life's unexpected blessings. Thank you for your compassionate wisdom."

Archangel Metatron

On Expectations:

Expectations should be structured yet flexible. I help you align your intentions with divine timing, ensuring your goals fit into the grand design of your life. Together, we'll refine your expectations so they uplift and empower you without limiting your spirit.

Talk to Me:

"Archangel Metatron, guide me to align my expectations with divine timing and purpose. Help me create a structure that supports growth and freedom. Thank you for your sacred insight."

Archangel Chamuel

On Expectations:

Expectations in relationships often stem from a longing for love. I help you nurture self-love so your expectations come from a place of abundance rather than need. Together, we'll create connections built on mutual respect and understanding, free of pressure.

Talk to Me:

"Archangel Chamuel, guide me to set loving and respectful expectations in my relationships. Help me root my hopes in self-love and confidence. Thank you for your tender guidance."

Archangel Samuel

On Expectations:

Expectations require vitality and energy to bring them to life. I help you approach them with balance, ensuring they don't deplete your spirit. Together, we'll cultivate enthusiasm and focus, allowing you to meet your expectations with strength and joy.

Talk to Me:

"Archangel Samuel, guide me to approach my expectations with energy and balance. Help me meet them with joy and vitality. Thank you for your empowering support."

Archangel Zachariel

On Expectations:

Unrealistic expectations can lead to frustration, but strength lies in adaptation. I help you confront challenges and recalibrate your hopes with resilience. Together, we'll transform rigid expectations into stepping stones toward growth and achievement.

Talk to Me:

"Archangel Zachariel, help me transform unrealistic expectations into opportunities for growth. Guide me with strength and perseverance. Thank you for your steadfast support."

Archangel Jophiel

On Expectations:

Expectations shine brightest when infused with gratitude and joy. I help you focus on the beauty of what you already have while setting hopeful, positive intentions for the future. Let your expectations grow from a place of light, not lack.

Talk to Me:

LIFE THROUGH ANGEL EYES

"Archangel Jophiel, help me set joyful and grateful expectations that reflect the beauty of my journey. Thank you for your uplifting presence."

Archangel Laviah

On Expectations:

Expectations often carry deep intuitive truths. I help you discern the subtle whispers of your soul, ensuring your expectations align with your inner wisdom. Together, we'll create intentions that feel authentic and divinely inspired.

Talk to Me:

"Archangel Laviah, guide me to listen to my intuition and align my expectations with my soul's wisdom. Thank you for your quiet insight."

Archangel Sandalphon

On Expectations:

Expectations have their own rhythm, much like music. I help you find the balance between anticipation and acceptance, ensuring your hopes align with divine harmony. Let your expectations flow with grace, like a melody unfolding perfectly in time.

Talk to Me:

"Archangel Sandalphon, guide me to balance my expectations with faith and harmony. Help me trust in life's perfect rhythm. Thank you for your grounding presence."

Archangel Jeremiel

On Expectations:

Reflection helps refine expectations. I guide you to review your hopes with compassion, showing you which ones serve your growth and which need releasing. Together, we'll create a vision for your future rooted in wisdom and positivity.

Talk to Me:

"Archangel Jeremiel, guide me to reflect on my expectations with clarity and compassion. Help me align them with my highest good. Thank you for your loving guidance."

Archangel Raguel

On Expectations:

Expectations in relationships thrive when balanced with harmony. I help you set fair and realistic hopes for yourself and others, ensuring mutual understanding. When conflict arises from unmet expectations, I bring peace and resolution.

Talk to Me:

"Archangel Raguel, guide me to create harmony in my expectations and relationships. Help me find peace when hopes are unmet. Thank you for your steady guidance."

Archangel Raziel

On Expectations:

Expectations hold divine mysteries, reflecting your spiritual journey. I help you uncover the deeper truths behind your hopes, ensuring they align with your soul's purpose. Trust me to transform your expectations into manifestations of universal wisdom.

Talk to Me:

"Archangel Raziel, help me uncover the spiritual truths behind my expectations and align them with divine wisdom. Thank you for your sacred insight."

Archangel Haniel

On Expectations:

Expectations require balance and grace. I help you find harmony between striving and surrendering, ensuring your hopes align with divine timing. Let me guide you to hold expectations lightly, trusting in the natural flow of life.

Talk to Me:

"Archangel Haniel, guide me to balance my expectations with trust and grace. Help me align my hopes with divine timing. Thank you for your gentle presence."

ON AGING FOR MEN

Archangel Michael

On Aging for Men:

Aging is a warrior's journey. It's not about losing strength but discovering a deeper, more enduring courage. I help you release fears of irrelevance or weakness and replace them with confidence in your evolving purpose. Each line on your face tells a story of battles fought and wisdom earned.

Talk to Me:

"Archangel Michael, guide me to embrace the courage and strength that come with aging. Help me honor the wisdom of my years. Thank you for your protection and clarity."

Archangel Gabriel

On Aging for Men:

Aging is a time for powerful expression. Your voice, seasoned by life's lessons, now carries a richer depth. I guide you to communicate your truth with confidence and joy, whether through spoken words, creativity, or by being an example to others. Your presence is an inspiration.

Talk to Me:

"Archangel Gabriel, guide me to use my voice and presence to inspire and uplift others as I age. Help me express my truth with wisdom and joy. Thank you for your guidance."

Archangel Raphael

LIFE THROUGH ANGEL EYES

On Aging for Men:

Your body may change with age, but it remains a sacred vessel. I am here to support you in nurturing it with care, offering healing for aches and the energy to continue living vibrantly. Aging is an opportunity to cherish your physical self and align it with your inner peace.

Talk to Me:

"Archangel Raphael, guide me in caring for my body as I age and help me embrace this phase with vitality and peace. Thank you for your healing touch."

Archangel Uriel

On Aging for Men:

Aging brings the gift of wisdom, born from a life well-lived. I help you see the purpose in every chapter of your journey and release fears of irrelevance. Embrace the tranquility and power that come from your experiences. Your light grows brighter as your years increase.

Talk to Me:

"Archangel Uriel, help me embrace the wisdom and peace that come with aging. Illuminate my path as I navigate this chapter of life. Thank you for your steady light."

Archangel Zadkiel

On Aging for Men:

The passing years can bring regret, but they also offer profound opportunities for forgiveness. I guide you to release any burdens of the past, finding comfort in the man you've become. Aging gracefully means making peace with yourself and embracing your life's wisdom with calm assurance.

Talk to Me:

"Archangel Zadkiel, help me forgive myself for the past and embrace the peace and wisdom aging brings. Thank you for your compassionate guidance."

Archangel Metatron

On Aging for Men:

Aging is the soul's evolution. I help you see how the lessons of your life form a sacred blueprint for growth. As you age, your focus shifts from worldly concerns to higher awareness. Together, we'll uncover your spiritual path and ensure your legacy shines brightly.

Talk to Me:

"Archangel Metatron, guide me to see the spiritual purpose in my aging and align my journey with divine wisdom. Thank you for your sacred insight."

Archangel Chamuel

On Aging for Men:

Aging is not the loss of vitality but a deepening of self-love. I help you nurture your inner child, heal past wounds, and see your evolving self as worthy and whole. Embrace this stage of life with confidence and a heart full of peace.

Talk to Me:

LIFE THROUGH ANGEL EYES

"Archangel Chamuel, help me cultivate self-love and confidence as I age. Guide me to see the beauty in my evolving self. Thank you for your tender care."

Archangel Samuel

On Aging for Men:

Aging is a call to rejuvenate your spirit. I help you rediscover energy, passion, and purpose in this new phase of life. Sleep deeply, dream vividly, and awaken with renewed vitality. Together, we'll ensure your later years are filled with strength and fulfillment.

Talk to Me:

"Archangel Samuel, guide me to rediscover vitality and passion as I age. Help me live this chapter with energy and joy. Thank you for your empowering support."

Archangel Zachariel

On Aging for Men:

Aging requires resilience, both physical and emotional. I help you stand tall in the face of challenges, transforming them into opportunities for growth. With each passing year, your strength becomes a quiet, unshakable force that inspires those around you.

Talk to Me:

"Archangel Zachariel, guide me to find strength and resilience as I age. Help me embrace the challenges of this phase with grace. Thank you for your steady support."

Archangel Jophiel

On Aging for Men:

There is beauty in the passage of time. I help you see the light in your aging face, the grace in your movements, and the wisdom in your eyes. Gratitude for each moment you've lived transforms aging into a celebration of life.

Talk to Me:

"Archangel Jophiel, help me see the beauty and grace in my aging. Guide me to celebrate the wisdom and light within me. Thank you for your uplifting presence."

Archangel Laviah

On Aging for Men:

Aging is a time of reflection and dreams. I help you access the wisdom of your subconscious, guiding you through dreams and quiet moments to understand your life's greater purpose. In the stillness, the truth of your journey is revealed.

Talk to Me:

"Archangel Laviah, guide me to reflect on my journey and uncover deeper truths as I age. Help me find wisdom in my dreams. Thank you for your quiet insight."

Archangel Sandalphon

On Aging for Men:

Aging is like a melody, each note building on the last to create a life song. I help you find grounding in this rhythm, ensuring you remain connected to the earth while embracing the spiritual growth that aging brings. Move to this sacred beat with grace.

Talk to Me:

LIFE THROUGH ANGEL EYES

"Archangel Sandalphon, guide me to embrace the rhythm of my aging journey. Help me stay grounded and connected to life's melody. Thank you for your harmony."

Archangel Jeremiel

On Aging for Men:

Aging offers the chance to review and refine your life's purpose. I help you reflect on past choices with clarity, forgive yourself for any missteps, and plan for a fulfilling future. Aging is not an ending but a chance to realign with your highest potential.

Talk to Me:

"Archangel Jeremiel, guide me to reflect on my life with clarity and align my future with purpose as I age. Thank you for your loving encouragement."

Archangel Raguel

On Aging for Men:

Aging brings new dynamics to relationships. I help you find harmony and understanding with others as your roles evolve. Whether as a mentor, partner, or friend, your presence grows in wisdom and fairness. Let your interactions reflect the balance of a life well-lived.

Talk to Me:

"Archangel Raguel, help me foster harmony and understanding in my relationships as I age. Guide me to navigate these changes with fairness and grace. Thank you for your steady guidance."

Archangel Raziel

On Aging for Men:

Aging reveals the mysteries of existence. I help you tap into the spiritual insights gained over the years, connecting you with universal truths. Together, we'll uncover the divine purpose behind your journey, ensuring that every moment has meaning.

Talk to Me:

"Archangel Raziel, guide me to uncover the spiritual truths behind my aging journey. Help me see the divine purpose in my life. Thank you for your sacred insight."

Archangel Haniel

On Aging for Men:

Aging gracefully requires balance and acceptance. I help you navigate the emotional waves of growing older, finding harmony between the man you were and the man you are becoming. Aging is not loss; it is transformation into a deeper, more balanced self.

Talk to Me:

"Archangel Haniel, guide me to find emotional balance and acceptance as I age. Help me embrace the transformation with grace. Thank you for your gentle presence."

ON EMOTIONS FOR WOMEN AS THEY AGE

Archangel Michael

On Emotions for Women as They Age:

Emotions often feel overwhelming during life's transitions, but they are not weaknesses. They are signals of your inner strength. I help you stand tall, cutting through the fears and doubts that can cloud your journey. Let me protect your heart as you embrace the wisdom of your emotions with clarity.

Talk to Me:

"Archangel Michael, stand with me as I navigate the emotions of aging. Help me release fear and doubt, and embrace the strength in my feelings. Thank you for your unwavering courage."

Archangel Gabriel

On Emotions for Women as They Age:

Emotions are your soul's language, growing richer with age. I help you communicate them with grace, whether through words, art, or quiet moments of expression. Your emotions are treasures—allow them to connect you more deeply to yourself and the world. Let joy guide you, even in the midst of change.

Talk to Me:

"Archangel Gabriel, help me express my emotions with clarity and grace as I age. Guide me to channel them into joy and meaningful connections. Thank you for your inspiration."

CH JODI M DEHN

Archangel Raphael

On Emotions for Women as They Age:

Aging stirs emotions that can feel heavy, but they also hold opportunities for healing. I help soothe the aches of unresolved feelings, bringing peace to your heart. Embrace the chance to nurture your emotional well-being as deeply as you do your body. Healing comes in waves, and I am by your side.

Talk to Me:

"Archangel Raphael, help me heal the emotional wounds I carry as I age. Soothe my heart and guide me toward inner peace. Thank you for your tender care."

Archangel Uriel

On Emotions for Women as They Age:

Emotions can feel overwhelming, especially as the years bring new challenges and realizations. I help illuminate your path, showing you how each emotion contains wisdom. Through despair, hope is born; through fear, courage grows. Trust that every feeling is part of your evolution into greater peace.

Talk to Me:

"Archangel Uriel, guide me to see the wisdom within my emotions and help me find peace as I age. Thank you for your illuminating light."

Archangel Zadkiel

On Emotions for Women as They Age:

Emotions from the past often resurface with age, but they do not define you. I help you release guilt, regret, and sadness, replacing them with comfort and self-forgiveness. Aging is a chance to rewrite the emotional stories you've carried, finding wisdom in the chapters you've lived.

Talk to Me:

"Archangel Zadkiel, help me release the weight of past emotions and replace them with forgiveness and peace. Thank you for your loving guidance."

Archangel Metatron

On Emotions for Women as They Age:

Your emotions are part of a sacred blueprint, guiding you toward deeper understanding as you age. I help you see the spiritual connections within your feelings, showing how each one serves your growth. Together, we'll align your emotions with your soul's purpose, creating harmony in every stage of life.

Talk to Me:

"Archangel Metatron, help me understand the divine purpose within my emotions as I age. Align my heart with my soul's journey. Thank you for your sacred insight."

Archangel Chamuel

On Emotions for Women as They Age:

Aging brings an emotional journey of rediscovery. I help you nurture self-love, especially when doubts creep in. Together, we'll heal the wounds of abandonment or loss, ensuring your emotions become a source of strength. Embrace your inner child and find peace in the depth of your feelings.

Talk to Me:

"Archangel Chamuel, guide me to love myself fully and embrace the emotions of aging. Help me find peace and strength within. Thank you for your gentle presence."

Archangel Samuel

On Emotions for Women as They Age:

As life evolves, emotions like grief or uncertainty may feel heavier. I help you find vitality in the midst of change, ensuring you move through this phase with resilience. Sleep deeply, awaken refreshed, and trust that your emotions are part of life's beautiful rhythm.

Talk to Me:

"Archangel Samuel, help me find balance and energy as I navigate the emotions of aging. Guide me to rest, restore, and thrive. Thank you for your supportive presence."

Archangel Zachariel

On Emotions for Women as They Age:

Your emotions can feel overwhelming, but they hold the key to your inner strength. I help you transform frustration, sadness, or uncertainty into resilience. Let me remind you of your capacity to face life's changes with courage, growing stronger with each passing year.

Talk to Me:

LIFE THROUGH ANGEL EYES

"Archangel Zachariel, guide me to find strength within my emotions as I age. Help me embrace change with courage and grace. Thank you for your steadfast support."

Archangel Jophiel

On Emotions for Women as They Age:

Aging invites you to see the beauty in every emotion—joy, sadness, gratitude, or longing. I help you embrace the elegance of your feelings, showing how they deepen your appreciation of life. Your emotions are as radiant as you are; let them guide you to gratitude and light.

Talk to Me:

"Archangel Jophiel, help me see the beauty in my emotions and embrace the grace of aging. Thank you for your uplifting presence."

Archangel Laviah

On Emotions for Women as They Age:

Emotions hold dreams and insights that emerge with age. I help you listen to the quiet truths within your heart, guiding you to honor the wisdom they bring. Trust your intuition, and let your emotions lead you to the profound revelations that come with time.

Talk to Me:

"Archangel Laviah, guide me to honor the wisdom within my emotions and find clarity in their depths. Thank you for your intuitive guidance."

Archangel Sandalphon

On Emotions for Women as They Age:

Emotions are like music, flowing with rhythms that shift as you age. I help you find balance, grounding you when emotions feel chaotic and lifting you when they inspire. Let the melody of your emotions guide you to harmony and acceptance.

Talk to Me:

"Archangel Sandalphon, help me find harmony in the changing rhythms of my emotions as I age. Thank you for your grounding presence."

Archangel Jeremiel

On Emotions for Women as They Age:

Aging is a time for reflection, and emotions often reveal what needs healing. I help you review your life with compassion, guiding you to release old wounds and embrace new possibilities. Let your emotions be a map to a future filled with hope and renewal.

Talk to Me:

"Archangel Jeremiel, guide me to reflect on my emotions with compassion and help me find renewal as I age. Thank you for your loving guidance."

Archangel Raguel

On Emotions for Women as They Age:

Emotions can create misunderstandings, especially as relationships evolve with age. I help you bring harmony to your interactions, ensuring that your feelings are respected and understood. Together, we'll create balance, restoring peace to your emotional world.

Talk to Me:

LIFE THROUGH ANGEL EYES

"Archangel Raguel, guide me to foster understanding and harmony in my emotions as I age. Help me bring peace to my relationships. Thank you for your steady support."

Archangel Raziel

On Emotions for Women as They Age:

Emotions hold divine secrets, deepening as you grow older. I help you uncover the spiritual truths hidden within your feelings, transforming them into sources of wisdom. Trust that your emotions are keys to unlocking life's mysteries, aligning you with your soul's path.

Talk to Me:

"Archangel Raziel, help me uncover the spiritual truths within my emotions and align them with my soul's purpose. Thank you for your sacred insight."

Archangel Haniel

On Emotions for Women as They Age:

Emotions ebb and flow like the moon's cycles, especially as you age. I help you find balance between releasing old feelings and embracing new ones. Together, we'll navigate the waves of your emotions with grace, turning each one into a moment of harmony and self-discovery.

Talk to Me:

"Archangel Haniel, guide me to navigate my emotions with balance and grace as I age. Help me find harmony in my heart. Thank you for your gentle presence."

ON AWAKENING

Archangel Michael

On Awakening:

Awakening is the discovery of your true strength, your divine spark. It's a moment of clarity when illusions fall away, and you step boldly into your purpose. I will protect you as you shed fear and rise into your authentic self. Awakening is not always easy, but I will be your shield and sword, ensuring you stay the course. Trust in your power to embrace this transformation.

Talk to Me:

"Archangel Michael, guide me through my awakening with strength and courage. Help me release fear and stand boldly in my truth. Thank you for your unwavering protection."

Archangel Gabriel

On Awakening:

Awakening is the voice of your soul whispering its truth. It calls you to realign with your divine path and express your unique light. I will help you hear this call clearly, to communicate with your inner self and find joy in the process. Your awakening is your masterpiece, a story waiting to be told. Together, we will write it.

Talk to Me:

"Archangel Gabriel, help me hear the voice of my soul as I awaken. Guide me to express my truth with clarity and joy. Thank you for your inspiration."

LIFE THROUGH ANGEL EYES

Archangel Raphael

On Awakening:

Awakening is the healing of the soul, the mending of fractures you didn't know existed. As you awaken, old wounds rise to the surface to be soothed and released. I am here to guide you through this healing, reminding you that every pain has a purpose and every scar is a symbol of growth. Together, we will find wholeness.

Talk to Me:

"Archangel Raphael, help me heal as I awaken. Guide me to release old wounds and embrace the wholeness within. Thank you for your gentle care."

Archangel Uriel

On Awakening:

Awakening is the light of wisdom igniting within you. It's a process of moving through despair, fear, and uncertainty to uncover the truth of your divine essence. I illuminate the path ahead, showing you that every challenge is a step toward peace and understanding. Trust in the journey, and I will ensure you never lose your way.

Talk to Me:

"Archangel Uriel, light my path as I awaken. Help me find wisdom in every moment and peace in every step. Thank you for your illuminating guidance."

Archangel Zadkiel

On Awakening:

CH JODI M DEHN

Awakening is a shift in perspective, a choice to let go of what no longer serves you. It's the freedom found in forgiveness—of yourself, of others, of the past. I help you find discernment in this journey, guiding you to recognize what truly aligns with your highest good. With awakening comes calm, comfort, and clarity.

Talk to Me:

"Archangel Zadkiel, help me release what no longer serves me as I awaken. Guide me to discern truth and embrace forgiveness. Thank you for your loving wisdom."

Archangel Metatron

On Awakening:

Awakening is the remembrance of your divine connection, the spark of enlightenment within your soul. As you awaken, the chaos of the material world begins to settle, revealing the sacred geometry of your purpose. I will guide you to align with your higher self, helping you see the order within life's mysteries.

Talk to Me:

"Archangel Metatron, guide me to align with my higher self as I awaken. Help me see the divine patterns in my life. Thank you for your sacred wisdom."

Archangel Chamuel

On Awakening:

Awakening begins with love—for yourself, for others, and for the divine within. It is a journey of healing emotional wounds and rediscovering your inner peace. I help you open your heart to this

LIFE THROUGH ANGEL EYES

process, nurturing your inner child and guiding you to embrace every part of yourself. Awakening is the blossoming of your soul.

Talk to Me:

"Archangel Chamuel, guide me to awaken with self-love and peace. Help me embrace every part of my journey. Thank you for your nurturing presence."

Archangel Samuel

On Awakening:

Awakening is a revival, a rekindling of vitality within your spirit. It's the process of finding light even in darkness, of renewing your energy and joy. I am here to ensure you stay grounded during this transformation, offering you the rest and resilience you need to emerge stronger than ever.

Talk to Me:

"Archangel Samuel, guide me to awaken with vitality and strength. Help me rest and find renewal in this journey. Thank you for your steadfast support."

Archangel Zachariel

On Awakening:

Awakening requires strength—a strength born from facing life's challenges and choosing growth over stagnation. I help you confront destructive tendencies and transform them into building blocks for your future. Every emotion, every obstacle is an opportunity to awaken further into the power of your soul.

Talk to Me:

"Archangel Zachariel, guide me to find strength within my awakening. Help me transform challenges into growth. Thank you for your empowering presence."

Archangel Jophiel

On Awakening:

Awakening is the unveiling of life's beauty, even in moments of struggle. It is the realization that your soul is as radiant as the stars. I help you cultivate gratitude and see the brilliance in all things, including yourself. Awakening is not just a journey—it is an art, and you are its masterpiece.

Talk to Me:

"Archangel Jophiel, help me see the beauty in my awakening and embrace the radiance within me. Thank you for your inspiring light."

Archangel Laviah

On Awakening:

Awakening is the emergence of your intuition, the soft voice of your soul calling you home. It often arrives in dreams, revelations, or quiet moments of insight. I help you trust this voice, guiding you to awaken with clarity and confidence in the wisdom within.

Talk to Me:

"Archangel Laviah, guide me to trust my intuition as I awaken. Help me hear the wisdom within my soul. Thank you for your gentle guidance."

Archangel Sandalphon

On Awakening:

LIFE THROUGH ANGEL EYES

Awakening is the harmony of body, mind, and spirit coming together. Like music, it flows in its own time and rhythm. I help you stay grounded as you awaken, ensuring you remain steady as your spirit reaches new heights. Your awakening is a song—let it unfold in its perfect melody.

Talk to Me:

"Archangel Sandalphon, help me stay grounded as I awaken. Guide me to embrace the rhythm of my journey. Thank you for your harmonious presence."

Archangel Jeremiel

On Awakening:

Awakening is a moment of reflection, when the past aligns with the future to illuminate the present. I help you review your life with clarity, forgiving what needs release and planning for what comes next. Your awakening is the dawn of hope, a chance to rewrite your story with love.

Talk to Me:

"Archangel Jeremiel, guide me to reflect on my journey with clarity and hope as I awaken. Thank you for your compassionate light."

Archangel Raguel

On Awakening:

Awakening can bring misunderstandings with others as you change and grow. I help you navigate these shifts with harmony, ensuring your relationships remain balanced. Awakening is not meant to isolate you—it's an opportunity to connect more deeply with the people who align with your soul's truth.

Talk to Me:

"Archangel Raguel, help me bring harmony to my relationships as I awaken. Guide me to connect with those who support my growth. Thank you for your loving guidance."

Archangel Raziel

On Awakening:

Awakening is the unlocking of divine mysteries, a remembering of the sacred knowledge within your soul. I help you interpret the signs, dreams, and intuitions that guide you on this path. Trust that your awakening is part of the universe's grand design, and I am here to help you uncover its secrets.

Talk to Me:

"Archangel Raziel, guide me to uncover the divine truths within my awakening. Help me trust the mysteries of my journey. Thank you for your sacred wisdom."

Archangel Haniel

On Awakening:

Awakening is the balancing of your inner light and shadow, the harmonizing of emotions and logic. It's a dance of transformation, and I am here to help you move through it with grace. Trust the process, and let the cycles of life guide you to your fullest expression.

Talk to Me:

"Archangel Haniel, guide me to balance light and shadow as I awaken. Help me embrace this transformation with grace. Thank you for your loving presence."

ON PRIORITIES

Archangel Michael

On Priorities:

Setting priorities is about choosing what truly matters and protecting that choice with unwavering commitment. Too often, distractions lead you astray from your divine purpose. I am here to help you establish clear boundaries and defend your focus. When you align your priorities with your soul's truth, you step into your full power.

Talk to Me:

"Archangel Michael, guide me to prioritize what aligns with my soul's purpose. Help me set boundaries and protect my focus. Thank you for your strength."

Archangel Gabriel

On Priorities:

Your priorities reflect the story you're writing with your life. Are you giving your energy to things that inspire creativity and joy? Or are you burdened by obligations that dim your light? Let me help you organize your time and energy to express the divine message you are meant to share.

Talk to Me:

"Archangel Gabriel, help me create a life that reflects my true priorities. Guide me to use my time and energy to express my highest purpose. Thank you for your wisdom."

CH JODI M DEHN

Archangel Raphael

On Priorities:

When health—physical, emotional, or spiritual—is neglected, other priorities crumble. I am here to help you place your well-being at the top of your list. Self-care is not selfish; it is the foundation of a balanced life. Together, we'll create a rhythm that nurtures your body, mind, and soul.

Talk to Me:

"Archangel Raphael, help me prioritize my well-being. Guide me to care for my body, mind, and soul. Thank you for your healing presence."

Archangel Uriel

On Priorities:

When life feels overwhelming, it's a sign that your priorities need clarity. Let me illuminate the choices that lead to peace and wisdom. Not everything requires your attention; some things are best left behind. Trust me to help you focus on what truly serves your highest good.

Talk to Me:

"Archangel Uriel, bring clarity to my priorities. Help me focus on what leads to peace and wisdom. Thank you for your guiding light."

Archangel Zadkiel

On Priorities:

Discernment is key when setting priorities. Are your choices rooted in love, or are they shaped by fear or obligation? I will help you release guilt and align your priorities with your highest truth. Let go of what no longer serves you and find comfort in decisions that bring calm and balance.

Talk to Me:

"Archangel Zadkiel, guide me to prioritize with discernment and love. Help me release guilt and align with my truth. Thank you for your compassionate wisdom."

Archangel Metatron

On Priorities:

The priorities you set shape the path of your life's sacred geometry. Are they aligned with your higher self? I help you see the bigger picture, revealing how each choice impacts your spiritual growth. Together, we'll clear distractions and create a divine structure for your time and energy.

Talk to Me:

"Archangel Metatron, guide me to prioritize in alignment with my higher self. Help me structure my life for spiritual growth. Thank you for your divine clarity."

Archangel Chamuel

On Priorities:

True priorities come from the heart. Are you nurturing your relationships, your inner peace, and your self-love? Let me guide you to focus on what brings joy and emotional healing. When you prioritize love—both giving and receiving—you create harmony within and around you.

Talk to Me:

"Archangel Chamuel, help me prioritize love and harmony in my life. Guide me to focus on what nurtures my heart and soul. Thank you for your tender guidance."

Archangel Samuel

On Priorities:

In times of chaos, priorities keep you grounded. They are the anchors that bring stability and vitality to your life. I help you simplify, removing distractions and strengthening your focus. Together, we'll create a foundation that sustains your energy and purpose, even in turbulent times.

Talk to Me:

"Archangel Samuel, guide me to simplify and prioritize what truly matters. Help me stay grounded and energized. Thank you for your unwavering support."

Archangel Zachariel

On Priorities:

Strength is needed to prioritize effectively. It means saying no to what depletes you and yes to what builds you up. I will help you confront destructive tendencies that pull you away from your goals and realign your focus on what strengthens your spirit.

Talk to Me:

"Archangel Zachariel, help me find the strength to set healthy priorities. Guide me to focus on what empowers and uplifts me. Thank you for your guidance."

LIFE THROUGH ANGEL EYES

Archangel Jophiel

On Priorities:

Your priorities shape how you experience beauty in life. Are you dedicating time to what brings you joy, gratitude, and inspiration? I will help you clear the clutter—both mental and physical—so you can focus on what truly adds value and purpose to your life.

Talk to Me:

"Archangel Jophiel, help me focus on priorities that bring joy and beauty into my life. Thank you for your inspiring presence."

Archangel Laviah

On Priorities:

Priorities often emerge through moments of intuition and revelation. Trust the whispers of your soul—they will guide you to focus on what matters most. I help you connect with these inner truths, using dreams and insights to refine your path and focus.

Talk to Me:

"Archangel Laviah, guide me to trust my intuition as I set my priorities. Help me focus on the truths within my soul. Thank you for your gentle wisdom."

Archangel Sandalphon

On Priorities:

Life is a symphony, and priorities are the notes you choose to play. Are your actions in harmony with your purpose, or is the melody off-key? I will help you create balance, grounding you so that every decision resonates with divine harmony.

Talk to Me:

"Archangel Sandalphon, guide me to prioritize in harmony with my life's purpose. Help me create balance in all I do. Thank you for your steady guidance."

Archangel Jeremiel

On Priorities:

Reflect on your life: are your priorities bringing you closer to your dreams or keeping you stagnant? Awakening to what truly matters requires honesty and courage. I help you review your choices, release what holds you back, and plan for a brighter future rooted in your soul's desires.

Talk to Me:

"Archangel Jeremiel, help me reflect on my priorities and align them with my dreams. Guide me to release what no longer serves me. Thank you for your clarity."

Archangel Raguel

On Priorities:

When relationships become unbalanced, it's often a sign that priorities need realignment. I help you bring harmony to your connections, ensuring you invest your energy where it's truly valued. Prioritizing mutual respect and understanding strengthens bonds and creates lasting peace.

Talk to Me:

LIFE THROUGH ANGEL EYES

"Archangel Raguel, help me prioritize harmony and balance in my relationships. Guide me to nurture connections that align with my truth. Thank you for your loving guidance."

Archangel Raziel

On Priorities:

Your priorities are like keys that unlock the mysteries of your divine path. Are they aligned with your soul's highest purpose, or are they clouded by distractions? I help you access the wisdom within to set priorities that resonate with your spiritual calling.

Talk to Me:

"Archangel Raziel, guide me to align my priorities with my divine purpose. Help me unlock the wisdom within. Thank you for your sacred insight."

Archangel Haniel

On Priorities:

Prioritizing is an act of balance, a dance between logic and emotion. Are you giving equal attention to your inner needs and external demands? I help you find harmony, ensuring your priorities reflect both your practical goals and your soul's desires.

Talk to Me:

"Archangel Haniel, help me prioritize with balance and grace. Guide me to honor both my inner needs and external goals. Thank you for your gentle support."

ON BOUNDARIES

Archangel Michael

On Boundaries:

Boundaries are your sacred shield, protecting your time, energy, and heart. Without them, you risk becoming depleted and vulnerable to forces that drain your strength. I am here to guide you in creating firm yet compassionate boundaries. Say no when needed, and stand tall in the power of your truth.

Talk to Me:

"Archangel Michael, help me create and maintain boundaries that protect my energy and honor my truth. Thank you for your strength and guidance."

Archangel Gabriel

On Boundaries:

Boundaries in communication are essential. They allow you to speak your truth without fear and listen to others with clarity. When words overstep or wounds linger, I will help you reclaim your voice and navigate relationships with respect and grace.

Talk to Me:

"Archangel Gabriel, guide me in setting clear boundaries in my words and actions. Help me communicate with kindness and strength. Thank you for your wisdom."

Archangel Raphael

On Boundaries:

LIFE THROUGH ANGEL EYES

Healing begins with boundaries that nurture your body, mind, and spirit. Are you giving too much without replenishing yourself? I will help you create spaces for rest and self-care, teaching you that saying no to others is often saying yes to your health.

Talk to Me:

"Archangel Raphael, guide me to prioritize my well-being by setting healthy boundaries. Help me honor my need for rest and renewal. Thank you for your healing presence."

Archangel Uriel

On Boundaries:

When fear clouds your judgment, boundaries become blurred. I am here to help you find clarity and wisdom in your decisions. Trust your intuition to guide you in setting limits that bring peace and balance to your life. Remember, a calm mind is your strongest ally.

Talk to Me:

"Archangel Uriel, help me establish boundaries rooted in wisdom and clarity. Guide me to trust my intuition in protecting my peace. Thank you for your light."

Archangel Zadkiel

On Boundaries:

Boundaries are not walls but compassionate lines that foster mutual respect. They require forgiveness—of yourself and others—to be effective. I help you release guilt and set boundaries with calm, discerning energy. Let us create a space where love can flourish without sacrifice of self.

Talk to Me:

"Archangel Zadkiel, help me set boundaries with discernment and love. Guide me to release guilt and protect my peace. Thank you for your understanding."

Archangel Metatron

On Boundaries:

Your energy is sacred, and boundaries preserve the integrity of your spiritual path. I help you define the energetic spaces where your growth can flourish. Let go of distractions and allow me to guide you in aligning your life with your divine purpose.

Talk to Me:

"Archangel Metatron, guide me in creating spiritual and energetic boundaries. Help me stay focused on my divine purpose. Thank you for your insight."

Archangel Chamuel

On Boundaries:

Healthy boundaries nurture self-love and emotional well-being. Are you letting others take more than you're able to give? I help you recognize the value of your heart and teach you how to say no with grace. Let us protect the peace within you together.

Talk to Me:

"Archangel Chamuel, help me protect my heart with loving boundaries. Guide me to honor my emotional needs with kindness. Thank you for your care."

Archangel Samuel

LIFE THROUGH ANGEL EYES

On Boundaries:

Boundaries bring stability to relationships, work, and your inner world. Without them, chaos reigns. I help you establish structure in your life, reminding you that balance requires saying no to anything that disrupts your peace or vitality. Stand firm in your choices.

Talk to Me:

"Archangel Samuel, guide me in creating boundaries that bring stability and balance. Help me protect my energy and peace. Thank you for your support."

Archangel Zachariel

On Boundaries:

Boundaries require strength. Whether it's breaking free from toxic patterns or standing firm against destructive influences, I help you find the courage to protect what matters most. Together, we'll create a life where your spirit can thrive.

Talk to Me:

"Archangel Zachariel, grant me the strength to set boundaries that protect my soul and energy. Help me stand firm in my truth. Thank you for your guidance."

Archangel Jophiel

On Boundaries:

Boundaries are the framework for a beautiful life. Without them, clutter—emotional, mental, or physical—takes over. I help you clear the unnecessary and focus on what brings joy and fulfillment. Let me guide you in creating a life that reflects your inner radiance.

Talk to Me:

"Archangel Jophiel, help me create boundaries that bring beauty and joy into my life. Guide me to let go of what no longer serves me. Thank you for your inspiration."

Archangel Laviah

On Boundaries:

Boundaries can come through the quiet wisdom of intuition. When something feels wrong, trust that signal. I help you tune into the whispers of your soul, guiding you to create boundaries that honor your inner truths and protect your dreams.

Talk to Me:

"Archangel Laviah, guide me to listen to my intuition as I set boundaries. Help me honor the truth within. Thank you for your gentle wisdom."

Archangel Sandalphon

On Boundaries:

Just as music requires pauses between notes, your life needs boundaries to create harmony. Without them, the melody becomes overwhelming. I help you find balance and groundedness by establishing limits that protect your rhythm and flow. Together, we'll create harmony in your life.

Talk to Me:

"Archangel Sandalphon, help me create boundaries that bring balance and harmony to my life. Guide me to honor my rhythm. Thank you for your grounding presence."

LIFE THROUGH ANGEL EYES

Archangel Jeremiel

On Boundaries:

Reflect on your life: where have boundaries been too loose or too rigid? I help you see where adjustments are needed, teaching you to create space for growth and release what no longer fits. Boundaries are not fixed; they evolve as you do.

Talk to Me:

"Archangel Jeremiel, help me reflect on my boundaries and adjust them for my highest good. Guide me to create space for growth and peace. Thank you for your clarity."

Archangel Raguel

On Boundaries:

Healthy boundaries bring harmony to relationships. Misunderstandings and conflicts often arise when limits are unclear. I help you communicate your needs with love and ensure mutual respect in your connections. Let us restore balance to your relationships.

Talk to Me:

"Archangel Raguel, guide me to set boundaries that nurture harmony and respect in my relationships. Help me communicate my needs with love. Thank you for your wisdom."

Archangel Raziel

On Boundaries:

Your spiritual journey requires boundaries to protect your energy and focus. I help you access the wisdom within, teaching you to say no to what distracts you from your higher purpose. Boundaries are your gateway to spiritual clarity and strength.

Talk to Me:

"Archangel Raziel, help me create boundaries that protect my spiritual path and focus. Guide me with your sacred wisdom. Thank you for your insight."

Archangel Haniel

On Boundaries:

Boundaries are the bridge between balance and chaos. I help you tune into your emotions and recognize when limits are needed. Whether in relationships, work, or self-care, I guide you to honor your needs with grace and compassion.

Talk to Me:

"Archangel Haniel, guide me to create boundaries that bring balance to my life. Help me honor my emotions with compassion. Thank you for your gentle strength."

ON SOUL PURPOSE

Archangel Michael

On Soul Purpose:

Your soul purpose is a calling as ancient as your spirit, one that echoes through time and space. Often, fear and doubt obscure it, making you question your worth or path. I stand with you as your protector, cutting away confusion and shielding you from distractions. Your purpose is not something you must create; it is already within you. Together, we will unearth it, step by courageous step.

Talk to Me:

"Archangel Michael, shield me from fear and doubt as I seek my soul purpose. Help me stand strong and walk forward with confidence. Thank you for your steadfast guidance."

Archangel Gabriel

On Soul Purpose:

Your soul purpose often whispers through the creative flow, through the words you write, the ideas you dream, and the emotions you express. I can amplify that voice, turning whispers into clarity. Let me help you communicate with your inner self and embrace the joy that comes when you align with your true calling.

Talk to Me:

"Archangel Gabriel, help me hear my soul's purpose clearly and express it boldly. Guide me to embrace my calling with joy and creativity. Thank you for your light."

Archangel Raphael

On Soul Purpose:

Your soul purpose is tied to the healing of both yourself and others. When you step into alignment with it, you will feel lighter, freer, and whole. I will guide you to the spaces in your life that need healing so that you can better serve your purpose. Through this process, you will rediscover the divine gift within you.

Talk to Me:

"Archangel Raphael, guide me in healing what blocks me from my soul's purpose. Help me connect with the gifts I'm meant to share with the world. Thank you for your loving care."

Archangel Uriel

On Soul Purpose:

Your soul purpose is illuminated in moments of stillness and reflection, like a lantern in the fog. I am here to bring clarity when despair clouds your path or fear keeps you still. Trust the wisdom within you—it will guide you to the peace and fulfillment your soul craves.

Talk to Me:

"Archangel Uriel, light my way as I seek clarity about my soul purpose. Help me trust the wisdom within me and find peace on this journey. Thank you for your guidance."

Archangel Zadkiel

On Soul Purpose:

LIFE THROUGH ANGEL EYES

Your soul purpose is woven into the fabric of your life experiences. Even the moments of pain and doubt serve as teachers, shaping you for your mission. I can help you discern the lessons in your journey, forgive yourself and others, and approach your purpose with a calm and open heart.

Talk to Me:

"Archangel Zadkiel, help me discern the lessons that lead me to my soul's purpose. Guide me to release guilt and embrace my divine calling. Thank you for your wisdom."

Archangel Metatron

On Soul Purpose:

Your soul purpose is a part of the divine blueprint etched into your being. It's not something you need to chase; it's something you need to remember. Let me clear the clutter of self-doubt and worldly distractions so that you can see your unique purpose with crystal clarity.

Talk to Me:

"Archangel Metatron, clear the path to my soul's purpose and help me align with my divine blueprint. Thank you for your insight and illumination."

Archangel Chamuel

On Soul Purpose:

Your soul purpose is deeply tied to your heart's desires. When you live from a place of self-love and peace, your purpose naturally unfolds. I can guide you inward, helping you heal any wounds of abandonment or unworthiness that cloud your path. Trust the journey—it begins with love.

Talk to Me:

"Archangel Chamuel, guide me to open my heart and embrace the self-love I need to fulfill my soul's purpose. Thank you for your compassion and wisdom."

Archangel Samuel

On Soul Purpose:

Your soul purpose is a source of vitality. When you connect to it, you feel energized, motivated, and alive. I am here to help you rest when you are weary and to ignite your inner fire when you need momentum. Trust your instincts—they are guiding you toward your purpose.

Talk to Me:

"Archangel Samuel, help me find the energy and focus I need to pursue my soul's purpose. Guide me with clarity and strength. Thank you for your support."

Archangel Zachariel

On Soul Purpose:

Your soul purpose is often revealed in moments of struggle. Challenges sharpen your resolve and strengthen your spirit, preparing you to step fully into your mission. I can help you find the strength to overcome obstacles and recognize how they are shaping you for something greater.

Talk to Me:

LIFE THROUGH ANGEL EYES

"Archangel Zachariel, help me find strength in adversity and guide me toward my true purpose. Thank you for your unwavering presence."

Archangel Jophiel

On Soul Purpose:

Your soul purpose is illuminated through gratitude and a love for life's beauty. When you open your heart to the blessings around you, your true path becomes clear. Let me help you see the wonder in each step of the journey, even before the destination is revealed.

Talk to Me:

"Archangel Jophiel, help me see the beauty and blessings that lead me toward my soul's purpose. Thank you for your light and grace."

Archangel Laviah

On Soul Purpose:

Your soul purpose often speaks through dreams and intuition. The quiet moments of reflection and insight carry the seeds of your divine mission. Let me help you trust those inner whispers and uncover the truths that guide you toward your higher calling.

Talk to Me:

"Archangel Laviah, guide me to understand the dreams and intuitions that point me toward my soul's purpose. Thank you for your wisdom and gentle guidance."

Archangel Sandalphon

On Soul Purpose:

Your soul purpose is a melody unique to you. Sometimes, it's hidden beneath the noise of the world. Let me help you tune into the rhythm of your inner being and find the harmony that aligns you with your true path.

Talk to Me:

"Archangel Sandalphon, help me hear the melody of my soul's purpose and align with its rhythm. Thank you for grounding and guiding me."

Archangel Jeremiel

On Soul Purpose:

Your soul purpose is often revealed through reflection and renewal. As you look back on your journey, you will see the threads that connect your experiences to your mission. Let me help you release what no longer serves you and plan for the future with clarity and hope.

Talk to Me:

"Archangel Jeremiel, guide me as I reflect on my life and uncover the threads of my soul's purpose. Thank you for your clarity and hope."

Archangel Raguel

On Soul Purpose:

Your soul purpose thrives when relationships are balanced and harmonious. Often, it's through connection with others that you discover your mission. I am here to help you restore fairness and balance in your relationships so that you can focus on the divine calling within you.

LIFE THROUGH ANGEL EYES

Talk to Me:

"Archangel Raguel, help me bring balance to my relationships so that I can focus on my soul's purpose. Thank you for your support and wisdom."

Archangel Raziel

On Soul Purpose:

Your soul purpose is written in the mysteries of the universe, connected to past lives and divine wisdom. I can help you access the ancient knowledge within you and uncover the spiritual truths that guide your path. Trust that your purpose is sacred and deeply meaningful.

Talk to Me:

"Archangel Raziel, help me access the divine wisdom within me to uncover my soul's purpose. Thank you for your insight and spiritual guidance."

Archangel Haniel

On Soul Purpose:

Your soul purpose requires balance—a harmony between action and intuition, between giving and receiving. I can help you align with this delicate rhythm, restoring your inner peace so you can walk your path with grace. Trust that when you are in harmony, your purpose will reveal itself.

Talk to Me:

CH JODI M DEHN

"Archangel Haniel, help me find balance and grace as I seek my soul's purpose. Guide me with harmony and peace. Thank you for your loving care."

ON CLAIRES

Archangel Michael

On Claires:

The claires—clairvoyance, clairaudience, clairsentience, and more—are divine tools, meant to connect you to higher realms and to guide your path. Fear often blocks their development, causing you to doubt their validity. Let me cut through these fears, protect your energy, and strengthen your faith in your abilities. Trust that these gifts are sacred.

Talk to Me:

"Archangel Michael, shield me from fear and self-doubt as I open myself to the claires. Help me embrace these divine gifts with courage and clarity. Thank you for your protection."

Archangel Gabriel

On Claires:

Your claires are a form of communication from the divine. They may come as subtle whispers, vivid visions, or feelings you can't explain. Let me help you fine-tune your ability to receive these messages. I will guide you to discern their meaning and express them with confidence.

Talk to Me:

"Archangel Gabriel, help me hear and interpret the divine messages coming through my claires. Guide me in expressing them with clarity and truth. Thank you for your support."

CH JODI M DEHN

Archangel Raphael

On Claires:

The claires are channels of healing—for yourself and for others. As you open to them, they can soothe old wounds and bring insight into the energy surrounding you. I can help you clear energetic blockages that dull these gifts so that your intuitive channels can flow freely and purely.

Talk to Me:

"Archangel Raphael, help me heal the blocks that prevent my claires from shining. Guide me to use these gifts to bring healing and love to the world. Thank you for your care."

Archangel Uriel

On Claires:

The claires are illuminated pathways of divine wisdom. They guide you out of the shadows of doubt and into the light of knowing. When fear clouds your perception, I can bring peace and clarity. Let me help you discern divine insight from mental chatter, anchoring you in truth.

Talk to Me:

"Archangel Uriel, bring clarity and wisdom to my intuitive gifts. Help me trust the messages I receive and use them to guide myself and others. Thank you for your light."

Archangel Zadkiel

On Claires:

LIFE THROUGH ANGEL EYES

Your claires are like keys to higher understanding, but they require calm and discernment to use effectively. If you feel overwhelmed or unsure, I can bring peace to your heart and sharpen your ability to interpret these messages. Forgive yourself for doubting and embrace your gifts fully.

Talk to Me:

"Archangel Zadkiel, help me trust and understand the divine messages coming through my claires. Bring calm and clarity to my heart as I open to these gifts. Thank you for your wisdom."

Archangel Metatron

On Claires:

The claires are encoded in your soul's blueprint, a part of your divine mission. You are meant to use them as tools to bridge heaven and earth. Let me guide you in aligning with your higher self, clearing distractions, and strengthening your ability to connect with divine frequencies.

Talk to Me:

"Archangel Metatron, align me with my higher self so that I may fully activate and use my claires. Guide me in honoring these gifts as part of my purpose. Thank you for your insight."

Archangel Chamuel

On Claires:

Your claires are most powerful when rooted in love. If fear or self-doubt clouds their expression, turn inward and reconnect with your heart. I can help you heal emotional wounds that block these gifts and guide you to approach them with peace, self-love, and trust.

CH JODI M DEHN

Talk to Me:

"Archangel Chamuel, guide me to open my heart and embrace the claires with love and peace. Help me trust myself as I connect to the divine. Thank you for your compassion."

Archangel Samuel

On Claires:

The claires thrive when your body and spirit are in harmony. Proper rest, care, and mindfulness allow these gifts to grow stronger. I can help you nurture your energy, restore balance, and ignite the vitality you need to connect with divine messages clearly and effectively.

Talk to Me:

"Archangel Samuel, help me restore balance and energy so I can fully connect to my claires. Guide me in nurturing these gifts with care. Thank you for your gentle guidance."

Archangel Zachariel

On Claires:

The claires often emerge in times of struggle, showing you strength within yourself you never knew you had. They are tools for understanding challenges and transforming them into growth. Let me help you embrace these gifts and use them to overcome obstacles with clarity and resolve.

Talk to Me:

"Archangel Zachariel, help me see the strength within myself as I develop my claires. Guide me to use these gifts to transform challenges into opportunities. Thank you for your support."

LIFE THROUGH ANGEL EYES

Archangel Jophiel

On Claires:

The claires bring beauty and wonder to your spiritual journey. They allow you to see divine truth in all things, from the mundane to the miraculous. Let me help you recognize the beauty of these gifts and use them to manifest a deeper connection to the universe's wisdom.

Talk to Me:

"Archangel Jophiel, help me see the beauty and truth in the messages I receive through my claires. Guide me to use them to enrich my spiritual journey. Thank you for your light."

Archangel Laviah

On Claires:

Your claires are often revealed in dreams, intuitive nudges, and moments of deep reflection. They are the language of your higher self. I can guide you to trust the subtle ways these gifts appear and help you interpret the revelations they bring.

Talk to Me:

"Archangel Laviah, guide me to trust the intuitive messages I receive through my claires. Help me interpret them with clarity and understanding. Thank you for your insight."

Archangel Sandalphon

On Claires:

The claires are a symphony of divine communication. Each one plays a unique role in creating a harmonious connection between you and the heavens. I can help you ground these gifts in your everyday life so that they feel natural and aligned with your spiritual journey.

Talk to Me:

"Archangel Sandalphon, help me ground my claires and use them to create harmony in my life. Guide me to connect to the divine with ease and grace. Thank you for your wisdom."

Archangel Jeremiel

On Claires:

The claires often awaken during periods of transition, offering clarity and insight as you navigate change. Let me help you reflect on your journey and understand how these gifts are guiding you toward a brighter future. They are a divine compass, always pointing you toward growth and renewal.

Talk to Me:

"Archangel Jeremiel, guide me to trust the messages of my claires as I navigate change. Help me see how they lead me toward renewal and growth. Thank you for your guidance."

Archangel Raguel

On Claires:

The claires flourish when your relationships are balanced and harmonious. They often bring insights about others and help you navigate interactions with grace. I can guide you in using these gifts to create fairness and understanding in your connections.

Talk to Me:

LIFE THROUGH ANGEL EYES

"Archangel Raguel, help me use my claires to bring harmony and balance to my relationships. Guide me to interpret the messages I receive with fairness. Thank you for your wisdom."

Archangel Raziel

On Claires:

The claires are rooted in divine mysteries and ancient wisdom. They connect you to spiritual truths beyond what the eye can see. I can help you unlock the full potential of these gifts, guiding you to access higher realms of consciousness and sacred knowledge.

Talk to Me:

"Archangel Raziel, guide me to unlock the divine wisdom within my claires and access the spiritual truths they reveal. Thank you for your insight and guidance."

Archangel Haniel

On Claires:

The claires are best nurtured in a state of harmony and balance. They require both faith and patience to blossom fully. Let me guide you to embrace these gifts with grace, trusting that they will unfold in divine timing and bring you closer to your true self.

Talk to Me:

"Archangel Haniel, help me nurture my claires with patience and trust. Guide me to use them in balance and harmony. Thank you for your loving presence."

ON EGO TAMING

Archangel Michael

On Ego Taming:

The ego is like a shield—it seeks to protect you but often blocks your growth. When it becomes overbearing, it clouds your judgment, distorts your truth, and keeps you trapped in fear. I am here to help you cut through the illusions of ego. In surrendering the need to control, you open yourself to divine guidance and live authentically. Let me help you distinguish between confidence and pride, strength and stubbornness, truth and illusion.

Talk to Me:

"Archangel Michael, help me release the illusions of ego and step into my higher truth. Guide me to act from strength and authenticity. Thank you for your protection."

Archangel Gabriel

On Ego Taming:

The ego can stifle your ability to connect with others and express your truth. It thrives on insecurities, making you defensive or overcompensating. Let me help you balance your voice so it comes from love, not fear. I will guide you to communicate with humility, compassion, and clarity, allowing your relationships to flourish.

Talk to Me:

"Archangel Gabriel, guide my words and actions so they reflect love and humility, not ego. Help me express myself in a way that fosters connection and truth. Thank you for your wisdom."

LIFE THROUGH ANGEL EYES

Archangel Raphael

On Ego Taming:

The ego often serves as a mask for unhealed wounds. It overreacts when you feel vulnerable, keeping you from addressing the deeper pain beneath. Let me help you heal these wounds. When your heart is whole, your ego softens, and you can live with openness, trust, and love. Healing is the key to taming the ego.

Talk to Me:

"Archangel Raphael, heal the wounds that keep my ego in control. Help me release pain and open my heart to truth and love. Thank you for your compassion."

Archangel Uriel

On Ego Taming:

The ego feeds on fear and doubt, creating barriers between you and your wisdom. When you tame your ego, you step into a space of clarity and enlightenment. I can illuminate the path forward, helping you see past the ego's illusions. Peace comes when you trust your higher self, not the voice of the ego.

Talk to Me:

"Archangel Uriel, shine your light on the illusions of my ego. Help me find wisdom and clarity in my higher self. Thank you for your guidance."

Archangel Zadkiel

On Ego Taming:

The ego clings to past hurts and grudges, making forgiveness nearly impossible. It thrives on judgment and resistance, blocking the flow of divine love. Let me help you release the need to prove or defend yourself. Forgiveness, both of others and yourself, is the most powerful way to quiet the ego's grip.

Talk to Me:

"Archangel Zadkiel, guide me to release judgment and embrace forgiveness. Help me free myself from the ego's hold and find peace. Thank you for your wisdom."

Archangel Metatron

On Ego Taming:

The ego is a challenge to master, but it's also a teacher. When balanced, it can help you stand in your power without arrogance. I can guide you to recognize the role your ego plays in your spiritual journey. Together, we will align your soul's purpose with humility and divine strength.

Talk to Me:

"Archangel Metatron, help me balance my ego and use it as a tool for growth. Align me with my higher purpose and divine truth. Thank you for your insight."

Archangel Chamuel

On Ego Taming:

The ego often masks a fear of abandonment or rejection, leading you to push others away or demand validation. Let me help you reconnect with self-love. When you nurture your inner child and feel whole within yourself, the ego's defenses fade, replaced by love, peace, and healthy relationships.

Talk to Me:

"Archangel Chamuel, guide me to heal my heart and find love within myself. Help me release the ego's fears and replace them with peace. Thank you for your gentle presence."

Archangel Samuel

On Ego Taming:

An overactive ego drains your vitality, creating unnecessary conflict and resistance. Let me help you find balance, restore your energy, and soften the ego's control. Together, we will focus on the present moment, where the ego cannot thrive. Peace and vitality come when the ego is quiet.

Talk to Me:

"Archangel Samuel, help me release the tension and conflict my ego creates. Restore my energy and guide me to live in harmony. Thank you for your care."

Archangel Zachariel

On Ego Taming:

The ego often emerges during challenges, driving you to react impulsively or defensively. Let me help you find strength and clarity, even in difficult moments. When you tame the ego, you can face obstacles with wisdom, turning problems into opportunities for growth and transformation.

Talk to Me:

"Archangel Zachariel, guide me to find strength beyond my ego. Help me transform challenges into growth. Thank you for your support."

Archangel Jophiel

On Ego Taming:

The ego can distort your perception, making you focus on flaws or chase superficial goals. Let me help you see the beauty and truth within yourself and the world. When you shift your perspective, the ego fades, replaced by gratitude, clarity, and love.

Talk to Me:

"Archangel Jophiel, help me see the beauty and truth in all things, especially within myself. Guide me to quiet the ego with gratitude and clarity. Thank you for your light."

Archangel Laviah

On Ego Taming:

The ego often clouds your intuition, filling your mind with doubts and distractions. In dreams and moments of stillness, I can help you reconnect with your higher self. Trust your inner knowing and let go of the ego's need for control. Peace comes when you listen to your soul.

Talk to Me:

"Archangel Laviah, guide me to quiet my ego and trust my intuition. Help me hear the voice of my soul and find peace. Thank you for your insight."

Archangel Sandalphon

LIFE THROUGH ANGEL EYES

On Ego Taming:

The ego thrives in chaos and disconnection. Through grounding practices like music, movement, or prayer, you can calm its noise and find harmony. Let me guide you to reconnect with the earth and your divine essence, creating a balance that softens the ego's grip.

Talk to Me:

"Archangel Sandalphon, help me ground myself and quiet the noise of my ego. Guide me to find harmony and balance. Thank you for your grounding presence."

Archangel Jeremiel

On Ego Taming:

The ego resists reflection, fearing change and growth. Let me guide you in reviewing your life with compassion and honesty. By understanding your patterns and embracing transformation, you can transcend the ego's limitations and step into a more authentic, peaceful version of yourself.

Talk to Me:

"Archangel Jeremiel, help me reflect on my life with compassion and honesty. Guide me to grow beyond my ego's limits. Thank you for your wisdom."

Archangel Raguel

On Ego Taming:

The ego often fuels misunderstandings and conflict, seeking to dominate rather than connect. Let me help you find balance in your relationships, creating harmony and mutual respect. When you release the need to control, you invite peace and fairness into your life.

Talk to Me:

"Archangel Raguel, guide me to release control and create harmony in my relationships. Help me tame my ego and find balance. Thank you for your help."

Archangel Raziel

On Ego Taming:

The ego blocks access to divine mysteries, keeping you anchored in the material world. When you quiet its voice, you open yourself to spiritual truths and higher consciousness. Let me guide you to understand the deeper purpose of the ego and transcend its limitations to embrace divine wisdom.

Talk to Me:

"Archangel Raziel, help me understand the purpose of my ego and transcend its limitations. Guide me to access higher wisdom and spiritual truth. Thank you for your guidance."

Archangel Haniel

On Ego Taming:

The ego disrupts harmony, creating imbalance and inner conflict. Let me help you reconnect with your divine essence, where balance and peace reside. In this state, the ego naturally softens, allowing you to live in alignment with grace, love, and your highest self.

Talk to Me:

LIFE THROUGH ANGEL EYES

"Archangel Haniel, help me restore balance and harmony within myself. Guide me to soften my ego and live with grace and peace. Thank you for your light."

ON MEETING GOALS

Archangel Michael

On Meeting Goals:

Goals demand clarity, focus, and unwavering determination. Too often, fear and doubt creep in, whispering that you're not enough. I stand ready to cut away these illusions with my sword of truth. With me at your side, you will find the courage to stay on course and the strength to overcome any obstacle. Every step forward, no matter how small, brings you closer to your purpose.

Talk to Me:

"Archangel Michael, clear away my doubts and strengthen my resolve. Help me see the path clearly and give me courage to face every challenge. Thank you for your guidance."

Archangel Gabriel

On Meeting Goals:

Goals are dreams brought to life through communication and action. Do you hesitate to speak your desires aloud or share them with others? I can help you give voice to your aspirations, unlocking the creativity needed to move forward. Remember, your goals are the stories of your soul waiting to unfold.

Talk to Me:

"Archangel Gabriel, help me communicate my goals clearly to myself and others. Inspire me with creative solutions and the courage to act. Thank you for your wisdom."

LIFE THROUGH ANGEL EYES

Archangel Raphael

On Meeting Goals:

Often, goals fail because you're too hard on yourself, neglecting your well-being in the process. To achieve anything, you must nurture your body, mind, and spirit. Let me help you heal the self-doubt and stress that hinder your progress. When you feel whole, the journey toward your goals becomes joyful.

Talk to Me:

"Archangel Raphael, heal the blocks within me that slow my progress. Help me nurture myself so I can move toward my goals with energy and joy. Thank you for your care."

Archangel Uriel

On Meeting Goals:

When your mind is cluttered with fear or indecision, goals seem far away. I am the keeper of wisdom, the light that shines on your path. Let me help you organize your thoughts and find practical solutions. The clarity you seek is already within you; together, we will bring it to light.

Talk to Me:

"Archangel Uriel, illuminate my path and help me find the wisdom and clarity I need to achieve my goals. Thank you for your light."

Archangel Zadkiel

On Meeting Goals:

Self-forgiveness is often the missing key to achieving your goals. Do you carry guilt over past mistakes or fear of failure? These emotions cloud your progress. Let me help you release judgment of yourself and others, replacing it with hope and wisdom. When you forgive, you free yourself to move forward.

Talk to Me:

"Archangel Zadkiel, help me release guilt and embrace forgiveness. Clear the emotional blocks that keep me from achieving my goals. Thank you for your loving guidance."

Archangel Metatron

On Meeting Goals:

You are capable of more than you realize. When your goals feel overwhelming, it's often because you've forgotten the divine spark within you. I work with the sacred geometry of creation, aligning your energy with higher realms of potential. Let me show you how to break your goals into meaningful steps, guided by divine purpose.

Talk to Me:

"Archangel Metatron, help me align with my highest potential. Guide me in creating steps toward my goals that are meaningful and inspired. Thank you for your insight."

Archangel Chamuel

On Meeting Goals:

Many goals are driven by a desire for love, acceptance, or peace. Yet, the true power to achieve lies within self-love. I can help you connect with your inner worth, so you approach your goals from a place of strength, not lack. When you believe in yourself, no goal is unreachable.

LIFE THROUGH ANGEL EYES

Talk to Me:

"Archangel Chamuel, help me embrace self-love and confidence. Guide me to pursue my goals with peace and strength. Thank you for your gentle support."

Archangel Samuel

On Meeting Goals:

Goals require energy, both physical and emotional. If you're feeling drained, it's time to reconnect with your vitality. Let me help you restore balance to your body and soul. With renewed strength, you can face your goals with determination and endurance, taking steady steps toward success.

Talk to Me:

"Archangel Samuel, restore my energy and help me maintain focus on my goals. Strengthen my determination and guide me with care. Thank you for your support."

Archangel Zachariel

On Meeting Goals:

Every goal brings challenges, but challenges are the crucibles where strength is forged. Do not shy away from the hard parts of the journey. Let me help you find resilience and power in the face of adversity. Each challenge overcome is a step closer to your destination.

Talk to Me:

"Archangel Zachariel, help me find strength in every challenge and perseverance in every setback. Guide me to meet my goals with courage. Thank you for your encouragement."

Archangel Jophiel

On Meeting Goals:

Goals are easier to reach when you see the beauty and joy in the process, not just the outcome. Let me help you shift your perspective so that every small victory feels significant. Gratitude and positivity will illuminate your path and make even the hardest tasks feel lighter.

Talk to Me:

"Archangel Jophiel, help me find joy and gratitude in every step of my journey. Show me the beauty in the process of achieving my goals. Thank you for your light."

Archangel Laviah

On Meeting Goals:

Dreams hold the seeds of your goals. Pay attention to the symbols and messages in your quiet moments. I am here to help you trust your intuition and the guidance that comes through dreams. Your subconscious holds the map; together, we will read it clearly.

Talk to Me:

"Archangel Laviah, help me trust my intuition and dreams as guides toward my goals. Show me the hidden messages that light my path. Thank you for your wisdom."

Archangel Sandalphon

On Meeting Goals:

LIFE THROUGH ANGEL EYES

Goals thrive on rhythm and grounding. When you feel overwhelmed, reconnect with the earth, music, or prayer to steady yourself. I can help you establish a foundation of calm, where your goals can grow naturally, one harmonious step at a time.

Talk to Me:

"Archangel Sandalphon, guide me to find grounding and harmony as I work toward my goals. Help me move forward with rhythm and calm. Thank you for your grounding presence."

Archangel Jeremiel

On Meeting Goals:

Reflect on where you've been to understand where you're going. Have past choices served your highest good? Let me help you review your life with clarity and compassion. Together, we can align your goals with your soul's purpose, creating a path that feels right and true.

Talk to Me:

"Archangel Jeremiel, guide me in reflecting on my past to align my goals with my higher purpose. Help me move forward with clarity and confidence. Thank you for your insight."

Archangel Raguel

On Meeting Goals:

Harmony in your relationships can be key to achieving your goals. When conflict or misunderstanding arises, it can derail your focus. Let me help you create balance and cooperation with those around you. A supportive environment will help you reach your destination more easily.

Talk to Me:

"Archangel Raguel, bring harmony to my relationships and clear the path to my goals. Help me create an environment of support and understanding. Thank you for your guidance."

Archangel Raziel

On Meeting Goals:

Goals are not random; they are connected to your soul's purpose. I hold the mysteries of the universe and can help you see the spiritual significance of your desires. Let me guide you to align your goals with the divine blueprint of your life, ensuring every step you take is meaningful.

Talk to Me:

"Archangel Raziel, reveal the deeper meaning behind my goals and align them with my soul's purpose. Help me move forward with clarity and intention. Thank you for your divine guidance."

Archangel Haniel

On Meeting Goals:

Goals are like seeds planted in the soil of your emotions. If frustration or imbalance dominates your heart, the seeds may wither before they bloom. I can help you align your emotions with the cycles of the moon and the natural flow of your energy. With harmony and patience, your goals will grow steadily and flourish in their time. The process matters as much as the outcome, and I am here to help you find grace in both.

Talk to Me:

LIFE THROUGH ANGEL EYES

"Archangel Haniel, help me find emotional balance and harmony as I work toward my goals. Align my energy with the natural flow of life, so my intentions may flourish in their own time. Thank you for your gentle guidance."

ON LOSS OF SELF

Archangel Michael

On Loss of Self:

The loss of self often comes when fear and doubt overshadow your inner truth. You forget who you are because the world pushes you to be someone else. Let me cut through the noise. My sword will sever the ties to false identities and restore your connection to your authentic self. You are strong, courageous, and worthy. Trust in me, and I will help you stand firm in your true identity, free of illusions.

Talk to Me:

"Archangel Michael, cut away the lies and doubts that cloud my sense of self. Protect me as I reconnect with my inner truth. Thank you for guiding me to my authentic identity."

Archangel Gabriel

On Loss of Self:

When you've lost your sense of identity, it's often because your voice has been silenced—by others or even yourself. I am here to help you find your voice again. Speak your truth, even if it feels small or shaky at first. Your words hold the key to rediscovering who you are. Creativity, joy, and the power of self-expression will lead you home to yourself.

Talk to Me:

"Archangel Gabriel, help me find the courage to speak my truth and express myself fully. Guide me back to the joy of knowing who I am. Thank you for your gentle inspiration."

LIFE THROUGH ANGEL EYES

Archangel Raphael

On Loss of Self:

Losing yourself can feel like a deep wound, leaving you disconnected and adrift. Let me help you heal this wound. Together, we will soothe the ache of confusion and restore wholeness to your heart and mind. The pieces of you that feel scattered will return, gently and lovingly, when you nurture yourself with compassion and patience.

Talk to Me:

"Archangel Raphael, heal the wounds of my lost identity. Help me rediscover the wholeness within myself. Thank you for your tender care and healing presence."

Archangel Uriel

On Loss of Self:

When you lose your sense of self, it's because the light of your inner wisdom has been dimmed. But that light never truly goes out. I will help you ignite it again, illuminating your path back to clarity and purpose. Remember, who you are is not defined by external forces but by the eternal truth within you. Trust in that truth, and let it guide you.

Talk to Me:

"Archangel Uriel, rekindle the light of my inner wisdom. Help me see clearly who I am and guide me back to my true self. Thank you for your clarity and insight."

Archangel Zadkiel

On Loss of Self:

Losing your sense of self often stems from carrying too much of the past. Regrets, guilt, and expectations can weigh you down, clouding your view of who you truly are. Let me help you forgive—yourself and others. Through forgiveness, you will shed the layers of false identities and reconnect with the pure, radiant soul within you.

Talk to Me:

"Archangel Zadkiel, help me release the burdens of the past. Guide me in forgiving myself and others so I can rediscover my true identity. Thank you for your compassionate wisdom."

Archangel Metatron

On Loss of Self:

When you lose yourself, it's often because you've forgotten the divine spark within you. I work with the Akashic Records and sacred geometry to remind you of your soul's blueprint. You are a unique piece of creation, perfectly designed for your purpose. Let me guide you to rediscover your divine essence and live in alignment with your truth.

Talk to Me:

"Archangel Metatron, reconnect me to the divine plan within me. Help me see my unique place in creation and reclaim my sense of self. Thank you for your sacred guidance."

Archangel Chamuel

On Loss of Self:

When you've lost your identity, it's often because you've lost touch with self-love. Without love, you drift, searching for validation outside yourself. I can help you reconnect with your heart, your inner child, and the peace that comes from self-acceptance. With self-love as your foundation, your true self will emerge effortlessly.

Talk to Me:

"Archangel Chamuel, guide me back to self-love and acceptance. Help me rediscover my true self with gentleness and compassion. Thank you for your unwavering love."

Archangel Samuel

On Loss of Self:

Losing yourself can leave you exhausted, as if your vitality has drained away. You may feel disconnected from your passions and purpose. Let me help you regain your energy and rediscover the spark within you. As your vitality returns, so will your sense of who you are and what you're here to do.

Talk to Me:

"Archangel Samuel, restore my energy and help me reconnect with my passions and purpose. Guide me to rediscover my true self. Thank you for your strength and support."

Archangel Zachariel

On Loss of Self:

Loss of self is a crisis of strength. It feels as though the core of who you are has crumbled. But it hasn't—it's simply buried beneath doubt and fear. Let me help you rebuild, brick by brick, until you stand strong and unshaken in your identity. Strength is who you are, even when you don't feel it.

Talk to Me:

"Archangel Zachariel, give me the strength to rebuild my sense of self. Help me stand firm in who I truly am. Thank you for your empowering guidance."

Archangel Jophiel

On Loss of Self:

Sometimes, losing yourself happens because you forget the beauty within you. You get caught up in comparisons or negative self-talk, losing sight of your unique gifts. Let me help you see yourself with fresh eyes, filled with gratitude and wonder. When you recognize your inner beauty, your true self will shine.

Talk to Me:

"Archangel Jophiel, help me see the beauty within myself and rediscover the truth of who I am. Thank you for your uplifting light."

Archangel Laviah

On Loss of Self:

In the quiet of dreams, your true self whispers to you. When your waking identity feels lost, I will help you tune into the messages of your subconscious. Through intuition and revelation, you'll remember who you are. The answers are already within; let me guide you to hear them.

Talk to Me:

"Archangel Laviah, guide me through dreams and intuition to rediscover my true self. Help me trust the revelations of my soul. Thank you for your gentle wisdom."

Archangel Sandalphon

LIFE THROUGH ANGEL EYES

On Loss of Self:

Losing yourself often happens when you feel ungrounded or disconnected. Let me help you root yourself in the present moment. Through prayer, music, or nature, I can help you find your center again. When you're grounded, the confusion lifts, and your true self emerges naturally.

Talk to Me:

"Archangel Sandalphon, help me find grounding and connection to rediscover my sense of self. Thank you for your steady presence and peace."

Archangel Jeremiel

On Loss of Self:

Losing yourself can feel like being lost in the fog of your past. I am here to help you review your life with clarity and compassion. Together, we will make sense of the experiences that have shaped you and reconnect you with your purpose. Your true self has never left; it's waiting for you to see it again.

Talk to Me:

"Archangel Jeremiel, guide me in reflecting on my life with clarity and love. Help me reconnect with my true self and purpose. Thank you for your understanding."

Archangel Raguel

On Loss of Self:

Sometimes, losing yourself happens when relationships are out of balance. The expectations or judgments of others can overshadow your identity. Let me help you restore harmony in your connections and assert healthy boundaries. As balance returns, so will your sense of self.

Talk to Me:

"Archangel Raguel, bring harmony to my relationships and help me reclaim my identity. Thank you for your loving guidance."

Archangel Haniel

On Loss of Self:

The cycles of life can sometimes obscure your sense of identity. Emotions rise and fall, leaving you uncertain of who you are. I can help you find balance and harmony, embracing the natural rhythms of your soul. In this balance, you will rediscover your true essence, luminous and whole.

Talk to Me:

"Archangel Haniel, guide me to embrace balance and harmony within myself. Help me rediscover my true identity with grace. Thank you for your gentle support."

ON DREAMS

Archangel Michael

On Dreams:

Dreams are sacred spaces where fear has no place. As you sleep, I stand guard over your body and spirit, ensuring no harm comes to you. Nightmares may be the echoes of your worries, but I will shield you from their weight. Sleep deeply and trust that in the realm of dreams, you are safe. Let your mind rest, unburdened, and awaken renewed.

Talk to Me:

"Archangel Michael, protect me as I sleep. Help me release fear and allow my dreams to bring clarity and peace. Thank you for your guardianship."

Archangel Gabriel

On Dreams:

Dreams are messengers, whispers from your soul and the divine. They may carry symbols of hope, creativity, or truths you've yet to acknowledge. I will help you decipher their meanings, especially when they feel tangled or confusing. Trust your dreams; they are your connection to deeper insights and inspiration.

Talk to Me:

"Archangel Gabriel, help me understand the messages in my dreams. Guide me to clarity and inspiration through the language of the soul. Thank you for your wisdom."

Archangel Raphael

On Dreams:

In dreams, healing flows freely. As you sleep, your body and spirit release the tension of the day, inviting restoration. I work within this sacred stillness, soothing wounds and renewing vitality. Whether physical or emotional, trust that your healing continues as you dream. Rest, and allow your body and spirit to mend.

Talk to Me:

"Archangel Raphael, guide me to restorative sleep. Let my dreams bring healing and renewal to my body, mind, and soul. Thank you for your gentle care."

Archangel Uriel

On Dreams:

Dreams are where wisdom emerges, often hidden within symbols and subtle whispers. I will help you uncover the truths buried in your subconscious and guide you to answers that seem just out of reach in waking life. Let your dreams be a space of discovery and insight, revealing your path forward.

Talk to Me:

"Archangel Uriel, illuminate the wisdom hidden in my dreams. Help me see their meaning clearly and use their insights to guide my waking life. Thank you for your light."

Archangel Zadkiel

On Dreams:

LIFE THROUGH ANGEL EYES

Dreams are opportunities for emotional release and forgiveness. In the quiet of the night, your soul processes the burdens of the day, letting go of guilt, regret, or sorrow. I will guide you through this healing process, helping you awaken lighter and more at peace. Trust the gentle work of the night.

Talk to Me:

"Archangel Zadkiel, help my dreams bring me healing and release. Guide me in letting go of emotional burdens as I sleep. Thank you for your loving presence."

Archangel Metatron

On Dreams:

Dreams are a portal to higher realms, where your soul connects with divine knowledge. I work with the sacred geometry of your energy field to align your dreams with your spiritual path. Trust the visions you see in your sleep—they are a reflection of your highest potential and purpose.

Talk to Me:

"Archangel Metatron, align my dreams with my soul's purpose. Help me remember and understand the divine messages I receive as I sleep. Thank you for your sacred guidance."

Archangel Chamuel

On Dreams:

Dreams are where the heart speaks most clearly. They reveal your deepest longings, fears, and joys. I can help you use your dreams to heal your emotional wounds and reconnect with the love within you. In the quiet of sleep, your soul finds the peace it needs to thrive.

CH JODI M DEHN

Talk to Me:

"Archangel Chamuel, let my dreams bring me emotional healing and peace. Help me understand the messages my heart reveals in sleep. Thank you for your loving care."

Archangel Samuel

On Dreams:

Dreams are vital for restoring your energy and vitality. Through rest, your body and spirit regain their strength. If your sleep feels restless or heavy, I can help you find peace in the night. Trust that with each dream, you are recharging the essence of who you are.

Talk to Me:

"Archangel Samuel, guide me to restful sleep and vibrant dreams that restore my energy and strength. Thank you for your revitalizing presence."

Archangel Zachariel

On Dreams:

Dreams can feel chaotic, mirroring struggles or challenges in your waking life. I help you find strength and clarity, even in the most turbulent dreams. Together, we'll uncover the meaning in the confusion, allowing you to face your waking challenges with renewed courage and understanding.

Talk to Me:

"Archangel Zachariel, help me find strength and understanding in my dreams. Guide me through their messages so I can face my days with clarity and courage. Thank you for your support."

LIFE THROUGH ANGEL EYES

Archangel Jophiel

On Dreams:

Dreams are a canvas for your mind and soul to paint possibilities. I bring beauty and clarity to these visions, showing you the grace that exists in your life and potential. Even in sleep, I guide you to see the beauty within yourself and your journey. Let your dreams inspire you.

Talk to Me:

"Archangel Jophiel, fill my dreams with clarity and beauty. Help me awaken with inspiration and a deeper appreciation for my path. Thank you for your uplifting light."

Archangel Laviah

On Dreams:

Dreams are my realm. I help you tap into the intuitive and prophetic messages hidden in the dream world. Each night, your soul speaks its truth, showing you glimpses of possibilities and warnings. Trust me to help you remember and interpret your dreams, turning them into tools for growth.

Talk to Me:

"Archangel Laviah, help me remember and interpret the messages in my dreams. Guide me to use their wisdom in my waking life. Thank you for your insight."

Archangel Sandalphon

On Dreams:

Dreams have a rhythm, much like music. They rise and fall, creating harmonies that reflect your emotions and thoughts. I help ground you in this rhythm, ensuring that your sleep is restorative and your dreams flow with peace. Let the music of the night guide you to serenity and balance.

Talk to Me:

"Archangel Sandalphon, bring harmony and peace to my sleep. Let my dreams flow like a gentle melody, bringing me calm and balance. Thank you for your steady presence."

Archangel Jeremiel

On Dreams:

Dreams allow for reflection, offering you the chance to review your past and prepare for positive change. I guide you through this process, showing you where growth is possible and how to move forward. Trust your dreams—they are a tool for transformation and renewal.

Talk to Me:

"Archangel Jeremiel, guide me through my dreams to reflect on my past and find clarity for my future. Thank you for your insight and gentle support."

Archangel Raguel

On Dreams:

Dreams can bring resolution to conflicts, even those you're not fully aware of. In the night, your soul works to restore harmony, processing misunderstandings and emotional tensions. I will help ensure that your dreams bring clarity and peace, mending the invisible threads of connection in your life.

Talk to Me:

"Archangel Raguel, help my dreams bring resolution and harmony to my relationships. Guide me to clarity and peace as I sleep. Thank you for your loving guidance."

Archangel Haniel

On Dreams:

Dreams are deeply tied to your emotions, waxing and waning like the moon. When your feelings are in balance, your dreams flow with ease, offering comfort and insight. I help you find this emotional harmony so your dreams can guide and restore you, showing the beauty within yourself.

Talk to Me:

"Archangel Haniel, bring balance to my emotions so my dreams flow with peace and insight. Help me awaken with a sense of harmony. Thank you for your nurturing guidance."

ON MORAL COMPASS

Archangel Michael

On Moral Compass:

Your moral compass is the shield that protects your soul. It gives you the strength to make choices that align with truth and integrity, even in the face of adversity. When the path seems unclear, I am here to help you stand firm in what is right. Courage flows from knowing your inner values; I will bolster that courage when the world tests you. Your compass points to the divine within you—trust it to lead you.

Talk to Me:

"Archangel Michael, help me stay true to my values. Guide me to stand firm in what is right and align my actions with integrity. Thank you for your strength."

Archangel Gabriel

On Moral Compass:

Your moral compass is the voice of divine truth, quietly guiding you toward choices that honor your highest self. I am here to amplify that voice, especially when confusion clouds your judgment. Whether through your words or your actions, let your compass speak clearly, reflecting honesty and compassion. Trust its wisdom; it will never fail you.

Talk to Me:

LIFE THROUGH ANGEL EYES

"Archangel Gabriel, help me hear the voice of my moral compass clearly. Guide me to express truth and integrity in all I do. Thank you for your wisdom."

Archangel Raphael

On Moral Compass:

A well-aligned moral compass brings peace to the soul. When you act in harmony with your values, healing flows naturally into your life and relationships. I help you find balance between heart and mind so your choices reflect your truest intentions. Let your moral compass be a guide to inner and outer wellness.

Talk to Me:

"Archangel Raphael, help me find balance in my decisions and align my actions with my highest good. Thank you for guiding me to live in harmony."

Archangel Uriel

On Moral Compass:

Your moral compass is the light of wisdom within you. It shows you the way when despair or uncertainty clouds your path. I will help you discern truth from illusion and guide you to choices that foster peace and understanding. When you follow your compass, you bring light not only to yourself but to the world.

Talk to Me:

"Archangel Uriel, illuminate my path with wisdom. Help me stay true to my values and act with clarity and purpose. Thank you for your guiding light."

CH JODI M DEHN

Archangel Zadkiel

On Moral Compass:

Your moral compass is a reflection of your soul's wisdom, and forgiveness plays a key role in keeping it aligned. When guilt or shame weighs you down, your compass may falter. I am here to help you release those burdens, making space for discernment and compassion. Through forgiveness, your inner guidance strengthens, leading you to live with integrity and peace.

Talk to Me:

"Archangel Zadkiel, help me release guilt and align with my inner wisdom. Guide me to make choices rooted in love and forgiveness. Thank you for your gentle support."

Archangel Metatron

On Moral Compass:

Your moral compass is an expression of your soul's sacred geometry, pointing you toward your divine purpose. I help you align your energy with your highest self, clearing away doubts and distractions. Trust your compass; it is your link to the greater cosmic plan, helping you live with clarity and purpose.

Talk to Me:

"Archangel Metatron, align my energy with my soul's purpose. Help me trust my inner compass and act in alignment with my highest truth. Thank you for your divine guidance."

Archangel Chamuel

On Moral Compass:

LIFE THROUGH ANGEL EYES

Your moral compass is a reflection of the love within you. When you nurture self-love, your compass becomes clearer, guiding you to choices that honor both yourself and others. I help you heal wounds of abandonment or self-doubt that might cloud your judgment. Trust in love—it always points true north.

Talk to Me:

"Archangel Chamuel, help me strengthen my self-love so my moral compass shines brightly. Guide me to act with compassion and integrity. Thank you for your love and care."

Archangel Samuel

On Moral Compass:

A clear moral compass gives you vitality, grounding you in your purpose. When life feels chaotic, your compass offers stability and direction. I help you find the inner strength to follow its guidance, even when the path is difficult. Trust that staying true to your values will restore your energy and sense of self.

Talk to Me:

"Archangel Samuel, help me stay grounded and follow my inner compass with strength and confidence. Thank you for your steady presence."

Archangel Zachariel

On Moral Compass:

When destructive tendencies threaten to pull you off course, your moral compass acts as a lifeline. I help you confront these inner battles with strength and clarity, ensuring your choices align with your greater purpose. Even when the journey feels challenging, trust your compass to guide you back to your path.

Talk to Me:

"Archangel Zachariel, help me overcome inner struggles and stay aligned with my values. Guide me to act with strength and purpose. Thank you for your protection."

Archangel Jophiel

On Moral Compass:

Your moral compass is a reminder of the beauty within you. When you honor your values, you align with the light of divine understanding. I will help you see the beauty in truth and guide you to choices that reflect gratitude, love, and integrity. Trust your compass to reveal the grace in each decision.

Talk to Me:

"Archangel Jophiel, help me see the beauty in my values and decisions. Guide me to act with grace and gratitude. Thank you for your uplifting light."

Archangel Laviah

On Moral Compass:

Your moral compass connects you to divine intuition, often speaking through dreams and subtle revelations. I help you attune to this quiet guidance, allowing your choices to reflect the wisdom of your soul. Trust the whispers of your compass, even when they challenge you to grow.

Talk to Me:

LIFE THROUGH ANGEL EYES

"Archangel Laviah, help me listen to the quiet wisdom of my inner compass. Guide me to make choices aligned with my higher self. Thank you for your insight."

Archangel Sandalphon

On Moral Compass:

Your moral compass creates harmony in your life, much like a well-tuned instrument. When your actions align with your values, the melody of your soul resonates beautifully. I will help you find this balance, ensuring your decisions reflect your truest self and bring peace to your journey.

Talk to Me:

"Archangel Sandalphon, guide me to act in harmony with my values. Help me create a life that reflects peace and integrity. Thank you for your steady support."

Archangel Jeremiel

On Moral Compass:

A moral compass allows you to review your life with clarity, learning from past actions and planning for a brighter future. I guide you through this reflection, helping you adjust your course when needed. Trust that your compass always points you toward growth and alignment with your highest good.

Talk to Me:

"Archangel Jeremiel, help me reflect on my actions and realign with my moral compass. Guide me to make choices that bring growth and peace. Thank you for your wisdom."

CH JODI M DEHN

Archangel Raguel

On Moral Compass:

Your moral compass brings harmony to your relationships and ensures fairness in your actions. When conflict arises, staying true to your values will restore balance and understanding. I will help you navigate challenging interactions with grace, ensuring your choices reflect kindness and integrity.

Talk to Me:

"Archangel Raguel, help me act with fairness and align my relationships with my values. Guide me to bring harmony to my interactions. Thank you for your guidance."

Archangel Haniel

On Moral Compass:

Your moral compass is deeply tied to your emotional balance. When your feelings are in harmony, your decisions naturally align with your values. I will help you find this balance, allowing your compass to guide you with clarity and confidence. Trust that your emotions and values work together to light your path.

Talk to Me:

"Archangel Haniel, help me find emotional balance so my moral compass shines brightly. Guide me to make choices rooted in harmony and truth. Thank you for your nurturing support."

ON OLD RELATIONSHIPS RESURFACING

Archangel Michael

On Old Relationships Resurfacing:

When past relationships reappear, it can feel like a battle between the familiar and the new. I help you set clear boundaries, protecting your present from the shadows of the past. Not all resurfacing relationships are meant to stay; some are lessons revisited, while others offer closure or a new beginning. Let me stand by your side as you discern whether to welcome them or release them.

Talk to Me:

"Archangel Michael, protect me as I navigate old relationships. Help me set boundaries that honor my growth and guide me to make choices that align with my highest good. Thank you for your unwavering strength."

Archangel Gabriel

On Old Relationships Resurfacing:

When someone from the past returns, it's a chance to reflect on how far you've come. I help you communicate your truth, expressing your needs with clarity and compassion. Old ties may bring a spark of creativity or the opportunity to forgive. Speak honestly, and trust that the right words will flow.

Talk to Me:

"Archangel Gabriel, help me express my truth clearly and navigate old relationships with grace. Guide me to communicate with love and honesty. Thank you for your wisdom."

Archangel Raphael

On Old Relationships Resurfacing:

Old relationships may resurface to heal wounds that were left open. I assist you in recognizing whether this reappearance is an opportunity for healing or a sign to protect your peace. Trust me to guide you toward decisions that nurture your emotional and physical well-being, leaving you stronger and more whole.

Talk to Me:

"Archangel Raphael, help me recognize the healing potential in old relationships. Guide me to make choices that protect my peace and foster growth. Thank you for your loving care."

Archangel Uriel

On Old Relationships Resurfacing:

When the past revisits, it can trigger fear or confusion. I offer you wisdom to see the higher purpose in this encounter. Is it a lesson, a blessing, or a moment of closure? With my guidance, you can find peace and clarity, ensuring this reappearance aligns with your soul's growth.

Talk to Me:

"Archangel Uriel, illuminate the purpose of this resurfacing relationship. Guide me to make wise and peaceful decisions that align with my growth. Thank you for your clarity."

LIFE THROUGH ANGEL EYES

Archangel Zadkiel

On Old Relationships Resurfacing:

Old relationships often reappear to offer forgiveness and closure. I help you release lingering pain, embrace compassion, and make decisions rooted in wisdom. Whether you rekindle or let go, I'll guide you to act with calm and discernment, freeing yourself from emotional burdens and opening the door to healing.

Talk to Me:

"Archangel Zadkiel, help me approach old relationships with forgiveness and wisdom. Guide me to release what no longer serves and embrace peace. Thank you for your comforting presence."

Archangel Metatron

On Old Relationships Resurfacing:

When old relationships return, it's often tied to a deeper soul pattern or karmic connection. I help you see the higher purpose behind these reappearances and align your response with your divine blueprint. Whether to move forward together or part ways, I guide you to act in alignment with your soul's purpose.

Talk to Me:

"Archangel Metatron, help me understand the higher purpose of this resurfacing connection. Guide me to act with clarity and align with my soul's path. Thank you for your divine insight."

Archangel Chamuel

On Old Relationships Resurfacing:

Old relationships resurface to teach us about love—self-love, forgiveness, or reconciliation. I guide you to honor your inner child and nurture the emotional healing these connections may bring. Not all relationships are meant to stay, but every one has a role in shaping your heart's journey. Trust the love within you.

Talk to Me:

"Archangel Chamuel, help me approach old relationships with self-love and understanding. Guide me to heal emotional wounds and embrace the lessons they bring. Thank you for your tender guidance."

Archangel Samuel

On Old Relationships Resurfacing:

The return of an old connection can bring both vitality and challenge. I help you discern whether this relationship revitalizes your spirit or drains your energy. Together, we'll focus on grounding you in the present while acknowledging the lessons of the past. Move forward with confidence and clarity.

Talk to Me:

"Archangel Samuel, guide me to discern whether this old relationship adds value to my life. Help me stay grounded and make choices that nourish my spirit. Thank you for your steady support."

Archangel Zachariel

On Old Relationships Resurfacing:

When someone from your past reappears, it can stir unresolved emotions or destructive tendencies. I offer you the strength to face these feelings with courage and honesty. Whether to rebuild or release, I help you confront what's hidden and choose a path that aligns with your inner strength and truth.

Talk to Me:

"Archangel Zachariel, give me the strength to face this resurfacing relationship with courage and honesty. Help me choose a path that reflects my growth. Thank you for your protective guidance."

Archangel Jophiel

On Old Relationships Resurfacing:

Old relationships can show you the beauty of growth. I help you find gratitude for the lessons they brought and clarity about their role in your life now. Whether rekindling or letting go, I'll guide you to honor the beauty in the journey, trusting in your inner wisdom.

Talk to Me:

"Archangel Jophiel, help me see the beauty in this connection and its lessons. Guide me to act with gratitude and clarity. Thank you for your uplifting presence."

Archangel Laviah

On Old Relationships Resurfacing:

The reappearance of an old relationship may be linked to dreams or revelations from the subconscious. I help you interpret the deeper meanings behind these connections and the emotions they evoke. Trust your intuition as it reveals whether this is a moment of closure, healing, or renewal.

Talk to Me:

"Archangel Laviah, help me understand the deeper meaning behind this resurfacing connection. Guide me to trust my intuition and make choices aligned with my growth. Thank you for your gentle wisdom."

Archangel Sandalphon

On Old Relationships Resurfacing:

Old relationships may resurface like a familiar melody, evoking memories and emotions. I help you find harmony amidst the noise, grounding your decisions in the present. Whether to let go or harmonize anew, I guide you to act with balance, ensuring your choices support your soul's rhythm.

Talk to Me:

"Archangel Sandalphon, help me find harmony as I navigate this old relationship. Guide me to make balanced choices that honor my growth. Thank you for your grounding presence."

Archangel Jeremiel

On Old Relationships Resurfacing:

When the past comes knocking, it's an invitation to review where you've been and where you're headed. I guide you to reflect on the lessons this connection offers and to plan for positive change. Whether you choose to embrace or release, trust the clarity that reflection brings.

Talk to Me:

"Archangel Jeremiel, help me reflect on this resurfacing connection with clarity and purpose. Guide me to make choices that lead to positive growth. Thank you for your guiding light."

LIFE THROUGH ANGEL EYES

Archangel Raguel

On Old Relationships Resurfacing:

The return of an old relationship may bring unresolved misunderstandings. I help you navigate these dynamics with fairness and balance, fostering harmony where it's needed. Whether to reconcile or part peacefully, I'll guide you to act in ways that restore equilibrium and honor your soul's truth.

Talk to Me:

"Archangel Raguel, help me navigate this connection with fairness and balance. Guide me to resolve misunderstandings and restore harmony. Thank you for your steady support."

Archangel Haniel

On Old Relationships Resurfacing:

Old relationships can evoke waves of emotion, from joy to disappointment. I help you balance these feelings, ensuring your choices are rooted in harmony. Trust me to guide you toward emotional clarity, whether to rekindle, forgive, or release. Let your intuition lead; it knows the way.

Talk to Me:

"Archangel Haniel, help me balance my emotions and navigate this resurfacing relationship with clarity. Guide me to act with harmony and trust my intuition. Thank you for your nurturing presence."

ON DISRESPECT AND LACK OF RESPECT

Archangel Michael

On Disrespect and Lack of Respect:

Disrespect chips away at confidence, leaving you feeling small. I stand as your shield, teaching you how to honor yourself in the face of others' disregard. I remind you that respect begins within—you must first set boundaries to show the world how to treat you. Call upon me when you need courage to stand tall and reclaim your dignity.

Talk to Me:

"Archangel Michael, help me establish firm boundaries and guide me to command respect in every interaction. Give me the strength to walk confidently in my truth. Thank you for your protection."

Archangel Gabriel

On Disrespect and Lack of Respect:

Disrespect often stems from misunderstandings or poor communication. I bring clarity to your words and help you express yourself with grace and conviction. When you feel unheard or undervalued, I assist you in speaking your truth with compassion, opening the door for others to see your worth.

Talk to Me:

"Archangel Gabriel, guide me to communicate clearly and confidently in situations of disrespect. Help me express myself in a way that fosters understanding. Thank you for your wisdom."

LIFE THROUGH ANGEL EYES

Archangel Raphael

On Disrespect and Lack of Respect:

Disrespect can wound the heart and leave scars that fester. I offer healing for the emotional pain caused by others' disregard. I help you forgive, not to condone the behavior, but to free yourself from the weight of resentment. Trust me to soothe your spirit and restore your inner peace.

Talk to Me:

"Archangel Raphael, heal the wounds caused by disrespect and help me let go of any resentment. Guide me toward forgiveness and inner peace. Thank you for your gentle care."

Archangel Uriel

On Disrespect and Lack of Respect:

Disrespect often triggers anger or despair, clouding your judgment. I bring wisdom to illuminate the true cause of these interactions—whether it's a lesson in patience, self-worth, or boundaries. Let me guide you to respond with dignity and grace, showing others the strength that lies in wisdom.

Talk to Me:

"Archangel Uriel, grant me the wisdom to understand and rise above disrespect. Help me respond with grace and maintain my sense of worth. Thank you for your guidance."

Archangel Zadkiel

On Disrespect and Lack of Respect:

Disrespect challenges your ability to remain calm and forgiving. I help you access compassion for yourself and others, even in difficult situations. With my guidance, you can discern whether to address the issue, walk away, or find peace within. Together, we'll turn discord into an opportunity for wisdom and grace.

Talk to Me:

"Archangel Zadkiel, help me remain calm and forgiving in the face of disrespect. Guide me to act with discernment and strength. Thank you for your steady presence."

Archangel Metatron

On Disrespect and Lack of Respect:

Disrespect can challenge your self-esteem and throw you off your spiritual path. I help you see these interactions from a higher perspective, reminding you of your divine worth. With my guidance, you can rise above petty behavior and realign with your soul's purpose, shining brightly despite others' shadows.

Talk to Me:

"Archangel Metatron, remind me of my divine worth and help me rise above disrespect. Guide me to stay aligned with my higher purpose. Thank you for your insight."

Archangel Chamuel

On Disrespect and Lack of Respect:

Disrespect cuts deeply, often triggering feelings of abandonment or unworthiness. I help you reconnect with your self-love, so others' actions no longer define your worth. Let me hold your heart and guide you to find peace within, ensuring you treat yourself with the respect you deserve, no matter how others behave.

Talk to Me:

"Archangel Chamuel, help me heal from the pain of disrespect and reconnect with my self-love. Guide me to find peace within myself. Thank you for your tender care."

Archangel Samuel

On Disrespect and Lack of Respect:

Disrespect can drain your energy, leaving you feeling depleted and unmotivated. I restore your vitality and guide you to let go of the emotional toll such interactions bring. Together, we'll focus on rebuilding your strength, ensuring you have the confidence and resilience to face the world anew.

Talk to Me:

"Archangel Samuel, restore my energy and help me let go of the emotional toll of disrespect. Guide me to move forward with strength and confidence. Thank you for your support."

Archangel Zachariel

On Disrespect and Lack of Respect:

Disrespect can stir destructive tendencies, tempting you to respond with anger or bitterness. I help you channel that energy into constructive actions, reminding you of your inner strength. With my guidance, you can address disrespect firmly but calmly, staying true to your values and avoiding harm to yourself or others.

Talk to Me:

"Archangel Zachariel, help me transform the anger from disrespect into strength and constructive action. Guide me to respond in ways that honor my integrity. Thank you for your empowering presence."

Archangel Jophiel

On Disrespect and Lack of Respect:

Disrespect can make you doubt your beauty and worth. I remind you to see the goodness within yourself and your surroundings, even when others fail to acknowledge it. Let me help you cultivate gratitude and self-respect, shining light on the beauty that disrespect can never diminish.

Talk to Me:

"Archangel Jophiel, help me see the beauty and worth within myself, even in the face of disrespect. Guide me to rise above negativity and hold onto gratitude. Thank you for your inspiration."

Archangel Laviah

On Disrespect and Lack of Respect:

Disrespect can reveal hidden truths about yourself and others. I help you explore the deeper meaning behind these interactions, often through dreams or intuitive insights. Trust the revelations that come as I guide you to understand the lessons within, using them to grow and strengthen your self-respect.

Talk to Me:

"Archangel Laviah, help me uncover the deeper meaning behind disrespectful interactions. Guide me through dreams and intuition to grow from these experiences. Thank you for your wisdom."

LIFE THROUGH ANGEL EYES

Archangel Sandalphon

On Disrespect and Lack of Respect:

Disrespect can feel like noise disrupting your inner harmony. I help you find grounding and balance, like a melody that restores peace. When others act out of tune, I guide you to remain steady, rooted in your truth, and focused on the rhythm of your own well-being.

Talk to Me:

"Archangel Sandalphon, help me stay grounded and balanced when faced with disrespect. Guide me to maintain inner harmony and strength. Thank you for your steady presence."

Archangel Jeremiel

On Disrespect and Lack of Respect:

Disrespect can be an opportunity for reflection, a chance to evaluate how you allow others to treat you. I guide you to review these moments with clarity, planning for change if needed. Together, we'll turn these experiences into stepping stones for personal growth and emotional healing.

Talk to Me:

"Archangel Jeremiel, help me reflect on experiences of disrespect and guide me to grow from them. Show me how to turn challenges into lessons. Thank you for your clarity."

Archangel Raguel

On Disrespect and Lack of Respect:

Disrespect often stems from imbalance in relationships. I help you restore fairness and harmony, ensuring that interactions honor your dignity. Whether it's advocating for yourself or mending a misunderstanding, I guide you to seek justice and fairness, always rooted in mutual respect.

Talk to Me:

"Archangel Raguel, guide me to restore fairness and harmony in situations of disrespect. Help me stand firm in my dignity and seek respectful resolution. Thank you for your support."

Archangel Haniel

On Disrespect and Lack of Respect:

Disrespect stirs emotions that can throw you off balance. I help you navigate these feelings, ensuring that your responses align with your inner harmony. Trust me to guide you toward a calm, balanced approach, one that allows you to maintain your grace and self-respect in any situation.

Talk to Me:

"Archangel Haniel, help me navigate the emotions caused by disrespect with balance and grace. Guide me to respond with strength and compassion. Thank you for your gentle guidance."

ON BUSINESS CONFLICTS

Archangel Michael

On Business Conflicts:

Conflicts in business test your resolve and integrity. I stand by you, sword in hand, to cut through the noise of fear, doubt, and uncertainty. When facing difficult decisions or power struggles, I help you set clear boundaries, act with courage, and stand firmly in what is right. Let no ego-driven battle shake your core purpose.

Talk to Me:

"Archangel Michael, guide me to face business conflicts with strength and honor. Help me establish boundaries and stand firm in truth and justice. Thank you for your unwavering protection."

Archangel Gabriel

On Business Conflicts:

Business conflicts often arise from unclear communication. I help you find the right words to clarify intentions, mediate misunderstandings, and restore trust. When dialogue feels impossible, I inspire creativity and solutions that bridge divides. With my guidance, your voice will be heard clearly and compassionately.

Talk to Me:

"Archangel Gabriel, help me communicate clearly and calmly through business conflicts. Grant me words that heal divides and inspire trust. Thank you for your divine guidance."

CH JODI M DEHN

Archangel Raphael

On Business Conflicts:

Tension and stress from business conflicts take a toll on your mind, body, and spirit. I offer healing to restore your balance and health amid difficult situations. I help you stay grounded in calm energy, seeing conflicts as opportunities for growth rather than sources of endless strain.

Talk to Me:

"Archangel Raphael, heal the stress and tension from business conflicts. Restore my clarity, peace, and well-being so I can face challenges with a calm heart. Thank you for your gentle care."

Archangel Uriel

On Business Conflicts:

Conflict clouds the mind, leaving you reactive instead of wise. I illuminate your path, helping you approach disagreements with insight and fairness. I give you the wisdom to see the root of the problem and offer solutions that restore harmony. Let me be your light through difficult conversations and decisions.

Talk to Me:

"Archangel Uriel, grant me wisdom to navigate business conflicts with clarity and fairness. Help me find solutions that honor all involved. Thank you for your divine light."

Archangel Zadkiel

On Business Conflicts:

LIFE THROUGH ANGEL EYES

In the heat of conflict, anger and frustration rise quickly. I guide you toward calm discernment and forgiveness, helping you see the bigger picture. Whether resolving disputes, forgiving mistakes, or learning from errors, I assist you in finding comfort and clarity, turning turmoil into valuable lessons.

Talk to Me:

"Archangel Zadkiel, help me find calm and clarity amid business conflicts. Guide me to act with discernment, forgive where needed, and move forward with wisdom. Thank you for your steady support."

Archangel Metatron

On Business Conflicts:

Business conflicts can disconnect you from your purpose and cloud your focus. I help you see the divine order in chaos, reconnecting you to your higher vision. Whether managing teams, leading with integrity, or inspiring cooperation, I bring clarity to realign your work with your soul's purpose.

Talk to Me:

"Archangel Metatron, guide me to rise above business conflicts and refocus on my purpose. Help me lead with clarity, wisdom, and higher vision. Thank you for your insight."

Archangel Chamuel

On Business Conflicts:

Business conflicts often create feelings of abandonment or loss. I help you restore peace and emotional balance, bringing compassion into tough situations. I guide you to nurture relationships, heal workplace divides, and handle challenges without losing sight of self-love and worth.

Talk to Me:

"Archangel Chamuel, restore harmony and peace amid business conflicts. Guide me to approach challenges with compassion and emotional balance. Thank you for your loving presence."

Archangel Samuel

On Business Conflicts:

Conflict drains your energy, leaving you overwhelmed and sleepless. I help you restore vitality, focus, and resilience to move through challenges productively. Whether it's managing stress or finding the stamina to persevere, I breathe new life into your work and help you find solutions that empower growth.

Talk to Me:

"Archangel Samuel, renew my energy and focus so I can face business conflicts with strength and purpose. Restore my balance and help me persevere. Thank you for your guidance."

Archangel Zachariel

On Business Conflicts:

When tempers flare, conflicts can lead to destructive actions. I guide you to harness your strength, directing frustration into productive solutions rather than harmful reactions. I remind you that calm strength and decisive action can resolve even the most stubborn divides.

Talk to Me:

LIFE THROUGH ANGEL EYES

"Archangel Zachariel, guide me to channel frustration into strength and positive action. Help me resolve conflicts with integrity and focus. Thank you for empowering me."

Archangel Jophiel

On Business Conflicts:

Conflicts in business can overshadow the good within yourself and your work. I help you refocus on beauty, gratitude, and the larger vision. With my guidance, you'll turn problems into stepping stones, finding inspiration to grow and move forward with renewed optimism.

Talk to Me:

"Archangel Jophiel, help me see the beauty and growth within challenges. Inspire me to rise above conflicts and focus on solutions with gratitude and clarity. Thank you for your light."

Archangel Laviah

On Business Conflicts:

Conflicts at work often carry deeper meanings. I help you uncover insights through intuition, dreams, and reflection, revealing the lessons within disagreements. By looking beneath the surface, I guide you to solutions that bring lasting understanding and peace.

Talk to Me:

"Archangel Laviah, guide me to understand the deeper meaning behind business conflicts. Reveal solutions through intuition and reflection. Thank you for your wisdom."

Archangel Sandalphon

On Business Conflicts:

When workplace tensions feel overwhelming, I ground you in stability and calm, like the steady rhythm of music. I help you maintain composure, ensuring your energy remains centered and unshaken. With me, you'll face challenges with quiet confidence and clarity.

Talk to Me:

"Archangel Sandalphon, ground me in calm and steady energy as I face business conflicts. Help me respond with confidence and centered focus. Thank you for your support."

Archangel Jeremiel

On Business Conflicts:

Conflicts call for reflection, a chance to step back and review the situation with clarity. I help you see where growth is needed, guiding you to plan steps for resolution and positive change. With patience and insight, you'll emerge from these challenges stronger and wiser.

Talk to Me:

"Archangel Jeremiel, help me reflect on business conflicts with clarity and understanding. Guide me to plan for resolution and growth. Thank you for your clear direction."

Archangel Raguel

On Business Conflicts:

Conflicts thrive when fairness and harmony are lost. I bring balance to disputes, ensuring justice and mutual respect prevail. I guide you to mediate with an open heart, seeking resolution that restores trust and strengthens professional relationships for the long term.

Talk to Me:

"Archangel Raguel, bring harmony and fairness to my business conflicts. Guide me to restore trust and resolve issues with justice and respect. Thank you for your support."

Archangel Haniel

On Business Conflicts:

Business conflicts stir emotions that disrupt harmony. I help you remain composed, balancing logic and intuition to address the heart of the matter. I guide you to lead with grace, ensuring your actions align with inner peace and wisdom.

Talk to Me:

"Archangel Haniel, help me find emotional balance and wisdom amid business conflicts. Guide me to act with calm grace and clear purpose. Thank you for your gentle guidance."

ON PERSONAL COMMUNICATION

Archangel Michael

On Personal Communication:

Your words carry power—speak with courage and truth. I empower you to express yourself confidently, set clear boundaries, and honor your voice. In difficult conversations, I stand with you, clearing away fear, doubt, and misunderstanding. Let me strengthen your resolve so you communicate boldly and authentically.

Talk to Me:

"Archangel Michael, guide me to communicate with courage, clarity, and strength. Help me express my truth without fear and establish boundaries that protect my peace. Thank you for standing by me."

Archangel Gabriel

On Personal Communication:

I am the angel of communication, inspiring your words to flow like a steady stream. Whether speaking, writing, or listening, I guide you to express yourself clearly and with joy. Let me help you deliver messages that uplift, clarify, and connect hearts, fostering deeper understanding and harmony.

Talk to Me:

"Archangel Gabriel, bless my words and guide my voice. Help me communicate with clarity, kindness, and purpose so I may connect meaningfully with others. Thank you for your divine inspiration."

LIFE THROUGH ANGEL EYES

Archangel Raphael

On Personal Communication:

Communication can wound or heal. I help you choose words that soothe rather than harm. When emotions run high, I calm your heart and guide you to speak with empathy and care. Let your conversations become bridges for healing, deepening trust and connection with those around you.

Talk to Me:

"Archangel Raphael, guide my words to heal and nurture relationships. Help me communicate with compassion, bringing understanding where hurt exists. Thank you for your healing presence."

Archangel Uriel

On Personal Communication:

Confusion and misunderstandings can cloud relationships. I bring wisdom to your communication, helping you find the right words and timing to speak. When fear holds you back, I illuminate the truth within, giving you the confidence to share your thoughts and listen with discernment.

Talk to Me:

"Archangel Uriel, shine your light upon my words. Help me communicate with wisdom, clarity, and purpose, dissolving confusion and misunderstandings. Thank you for your insight and guidance."

Archangel Zadkiel

On Personal Communication:

Communication falters without understanding and forgiveness. I help you listen without judgment, speak with patience, and forgive where pain lingers. Through gentle words and discernment, I guide you to navigate even the most difficult conversations with calm, restoring peace where it's needed.

Talk to Me:

"Archangel Zadkiel, help me communicate with patience, discernment, and forgiveness. Guide me to speak calmly and listen with an open heart. Thank you for helping me restore peace."

Archangel Metatron

On Personal Communication:

Your words shape reality—use them to create connections, not walls. I help you align your thoughts and voice with your highest truth. Whether teaching, leading, or sharing your vision, I guide you to communicate with clarity and intention, inspiring growth for yourself and others.

Talk to Me:

"Archangel Metatron, guide my thoughts and words to align with truth and purpose. Help me communicate in ways that inspire and uplift. Thank you for your divine wisdom."

Archangel Chamuel

On Personal Communication:

Communication can heal emotional wounds and bring relationships closer. I help you speak with love, vulnerability, and understanding.

LIFE THROUGH ANGEL EYES

Whether mending a rift, expressing feelings, or nurturing connections, I guide you to share from the heart, turning words into tools for deeper intimacy and trust.

Talk to Me:

"Archangel Chamuel, guide me to communicate from the heart with love and honesty. Help me nurture relationships through understanding and emotional connection. Thank you for your gentle support."

Archangel Samuel

On Personal Communication:

Tired minds and weary spirits struggle to connect meaningfully. I restore your energy and focus, allowing you to approach conversations with clarity and intention. I help you find the strength to communicate effectively, even in difficult moments, fostering healthier, more productive relationships.

Talk to Me:

"Archangel Samuel, restore my energy and focus so I can communicate clearly and purposefully. Help me share my thoughts with strength and intention. Thank you for revitalizing my spirit."

Archangel Zachariel

On Personal Communication:

In moments of conflict or misunderstanding, destructive words can harm relationships. I guide you to channel frustration into strength and choose constructive communication. Let me help you turn arguments into opportunities for growth, replacing harsh words with those that build bridges and strengthen connections.

Talk to Me:

"Archangel Zachariel, help me transform frustration into calm, constructive communication. Guide me to speak with strength, kindness, and purpose. Thank you for helping me grow."

Archangel Jophiel

On Personal Communication:

Communication flows best when seen through the lens of beauty and gratitude. I help you appreciate the goodness in yourself and others, guiding your words to reflect kindness and joy. Let your conversations become reminders of connection, understanding, and the beauty of human relationships.

Talk to Me:

"Archangel Jophiel, inspire me to communicate with gratitude, kindness, and grace. Help me see beauty in every interaction. Thank you for uplifting my spirit."

Archangel Laviah

On Personal Communication:

Sometimes the answers you seek lie in your dreams or intuition. I help you tune into your inner voice, guiding you to communicate truths you might otherwise overlook. Whether through reflection, quiet understanding, or deep conversations, I help you express what truly matters.

Talk to Me:

LIFE THROUGH ANGEL EYES

"Archangel Laviah, guide me to listen to my intuition and communicate my deeper truths. Help me share my thoughts with clarity and wisdom. Thank you for your insight."

Archangel Sandalphon

On Personal Communication:

Like music, personal communication flows best when in harmony. I ground you in calm energy, helping you stay centered even in challenging conversations. Whether speaking softly or listening deeply, I guide you to communicate with rhythm, balance, and heartfelt connection.

Talk to Me:

"Archangel Sandalphon, help me remain calm and grounded in communication. Guide me to speak and listen in harmony, bringing peace to every interaction. Thank you for your steady guidance."

Archangel Jeremiel

On Personal Communication:

Communication often requires reflection—understanding what needs to be said and when. I guide you to step back, review your words, and plan for conversations that bring positive change. I help you speak with clarity and intention, resolving issues through thoughtful understanding.

Talk to Me:

"Archangel Jeremiel, guide me to reflect on my communication and plan my words carefully. Help me speak with intention and clarity to inspire positive outcomes. Thank you for your wisdom."

CH JODI M DEHN

Archangel Raguel

On Personal Communication:

Harmonious relationships rely on fair, open communication. I guide you to resolve misunderstandings with justice and compassion. I help you speak truthfully and listen fairly, ensuring both sides are heard. Let me help you restore balance where communication has faltered.

Talk to Me:

"Archangel Raguel, guide me to communicate fairly, openly, and with compassion. Help me restore harmony and balance where misunderstandings arise. Thank you for your loving support."

Archangel Haniel

On Personal Communication:

Balanced communication stems from emotional awareness and calm. I help you express yourself gracefully, guiding you to remain centered in your feelings while honoring others'. I bring harmony to interactions, ensuring emotions don't cloud your message but instead enhance understanding and connection.

Talk to Me:

"Archangel Haniel, help me communicate with balance, grace, and emotional awareness. Guide me to express myself calmly and connect with others harmoniously. Thank you for your gentle guidance."

ON CAREER CHANGE

Archangel Michael

On Career Change:

Your courage is your compass. Career changes require bravery to leave behind the familiar and step into the unknown. I am here to protect and guide you, shielding you from fear and doubt. Trust in your abilities and divine guidance. With faith, you will find your path.

Talk to Me:

"Archangel Michael, grant me the courage to embrace change and pursue my career dreams. Protect me from fear and doubt as I take bold steps forward. Thank you for your unwavering strength."

Archangel Gabriel

On Career Change:

A career change is a story waiting to be written, and I am the angel of communication to help you articulate your dreams. Whether it's writing resumes, presenting your skills, or pursuing creative paths, I'll guide you to share your vision with clarity and confidence.

Talk to Me:

"Archangel Gabriel, inspire me to communicate my goals clearly and confidently. Help me navigate this transition with grace, creativity, and joy. Thank you for your guidance."

Archangel Raphael

On Career Change:

Transitions can be stressful, but healing and renewal lie within them. I bring you the calm to navigate the unknown and the energy to follow your calling. Your career is part of your healing journey—let me guide you to choices that nourish your soul and wellbeing.

Talk to Me:

"Archangel Raphael, bring me peace during this career shift. Guide me to choices that align with my purpose and well-being. Thank you for your healing light."

Archangel Uriel

On Career Change:

A career change is often born of dissatisfaction or an inner calling for something greater. I bring clarity and wisdom, helping you see beyond fear and into possibility. Let me illuminate the path and spark ideas that align with your soul's deeper purpose.

Talk to Me:

"Archangel Uriel, light my way as I explore new career possibilities. Bring me clarity and wisdom to make decisions that honor my soul's purpose. Thank you for your insight."

Archangel Zadkiel

On Career Change:

Career changes are opportunities for transformation. Release guilt, regret, or attachments to the past and embrace the freedom to grow. I bring discernment to help you choose wisely, and calm to make the process smoother. Your best decisions come from a place of self-forgiveness and trust.

LIFE THROUGH ANGEL EYES

Talk to Me:

"Archangel Zadkiel, help me release guilt and embrace transformation. Guide me to make career choices with wisdom and peace. Thank you for your comforting presence."

Archangel Metatron

On Career Change:

Every career shift is a chance to align with your divine blueprint. I help you connect with your higher self and recognize the steps needed for your spiritual and professional growth. Whether teaching, learning, or leading, let me guide you toward enlightenment in your next chapter.

Talk to Me:

"Archangel Metatron, guide me toward a career path that aligns with my highest potential. Help me connect with my divine purpose and make choices that uplift my spirit. Thank you for your light."

Archangel Chamuel

On Career Change:

Change can feel like abandonment—of your past or stability—but it's truly an act of self-love. I help you find inner peace as you step into a new role, balancing emotional growth with practical needs. Trust that your next path will heal and fulfill you.

Talk to Me:

"Archangel Chamuel, guide me to embrace this change with love and trust. Help me balance my emotions and find peace as I create a fulfilling career. Thank you for your gentle support."

CH JODI M DEHN

Archangel Samuel

On Career Change:

Sometimes, career change is born from burnout or exhaustion. I help restore your vitality, guiding you to find work that energizes rather than depletes. Together, we'll uncover paths that reignite your passion and bring balance back into your professional life.

Talk to Me:

"Archangel Samuel, restore my energy and passion for my career. Guide me to make changes that bring balance, fulfillment, and joy. Thank you for revitalizing my spirit."

Archangel Zachariel

On Career Change:

Leaving behind a secure role may feel like dismantling your foundations, but strength lies in growth. I help you break through doubts and destructive tendencies, giving you the courage to rebuild in ways that align with your highest potential. Step forward boldly—I am with you.

Talk to Me:

"Archangel Zachariel, help me overcome fear and doubt as I embrace change. Guide me to rebuild my career with strength and purpose. Thank you for your empowering presence."

Archangel Jophiel

On Career Change:

In transitions, beauty can be found in new beginnings. I help you see the blessings within uncertainty and manifest goals that align with

LIFE THROUGH ANGEL EYES

your highest joy. Shift your perspective to gratitude and possibility, and watch your dreams take shape with grace and understanding.

Talk to Me:

"Archangel Jophiel, show me the beauty in this transition. Help me manifest a career path filled with purpose and joy. Thank you for your loving light."

Archangel Laviah

On Career Change:

The answers to your career questions may come in dreams or moments of intuition. I help you tap into your subconscious, bringing clarity and revelations to guide your choices. Trust the wisdom within—you already know the way; I'll help you see it clearly.

Talk to Me:

"Archangel Laviah, guide my dreams and intuition as I navigate this change. Help me uncover the answers I seek and trust my inner wisdom. Thank you for your guidance."

Archangel Sandalphon

On Career Change:

Career shifts require groundedness amidst chaos. I help you stay centered, balancing ambition with inner peace. Like a steady rhythm, I guide you to take each step with confidence and grace, creating harmony between your goals and the life you're building.

Talk to Me:

"Archangel Sandalphon, ground me as I navigate this career transition. Help me move forward with balance, purpose, and peace. Thank you for your steady guidance."

Archangel Jeremiel

On Career Change:

Career changes invite reflection. Take stock of where you've been and where you want to go. I guide you to review past lessons, forgive yourself for any perceived mistakes, and plan a brighter future. Let's create a path filled with positive transformation.

Talk to Me:

"Archangel Jeremiel, help me reflect on my past and plan for a fulfilling future. Guide me to make choices that align with my highest good. Thank you for your wisdom."

Archangel Raguel

On Career Change:

Harmony in relationships is key during transitions. Whether negotiating with employers or seeking support from loved ones, I help you foster fairness and understanding. Let me guide you to resolve conflicts and build connections that support your career dreams.

Talk to Me:

"Archangel Raguel, help me navigate relationships during this career change with fairness and harmony. Guide me to communicate clearly and find support in my decisions. Thank you for your loving presence."

LIFE THROUGH ANGEL EYES

Archangel Haniel

On Career Change:

Career changes can stir deep emotions. I help you maintain balance, turning doubt into confidence and fear into excitement. By aligning your intuition with your choices, I guide you to a path that harmonizes your emotional, spiritual, and professional goals.

Talk to Me:

"Archangel Haniel, help me find balance and clarity as I embrace this career change. Guide me to trust my intuition and align with my highest purpose. Thank you for your gentle support."

ON AGING PARENTS

Archangel Michael

On Aging Parents:

Caring for aging parents calls for strength and clear boundaries. I am here to give you the courage to stand firm when decisions are hard and to protect your heart when emotions run high. Trust in your ability to safeguard their well-being while honoring your own. Let me shield you from guilt and fear, helping you act from a place of love and stability.

Talk to Me:

"Archangel Michael, strengthen me as I care for my aging parents. Help me set healthy boundaries and protect me from fear and guilt. Thank you for your unwavering guidance."

Archangel Gabriel

On Aging Parents:

This is a season for meaningful communication. I help you share your feelings and listen with compassion, even in the face of frustration or generational gaps. With my guidance, your words will carry love and clarity, deepening your connection during this tender time.

Talk to Me:

"Archangel Gabriel, help me express my love and concerns with gentleness and clarity. Guide our conversations so that they build understanding and connection. Thank you for your wisdom."

LIFE THROUGH ANGEL EYES

Archangel Raphael

On Aging Parents:

Physical care for aging parents can be draining, but it's also a profound act of healing. I bring soothing energy to ease their ailments and replenish your spirit. Trust that your hands and heart are instruments of love, and I'll guide you toward the support you both need.

Talk to Me:

"Archangel Raphael, bring healing and peace to my parents' lives. Replenish my energy and show me how to care for them in ways that honor their dignity and my well-being. Thank you for your light."

Archangel Uriel

On Aging Parents:

Navigating this stage often feels overwhelming, but I offer wisdom to help you make decisions with clarity. I bring calm to emotional turmoil and help you see the bigger picture—this time is an opportunity to honor your parents' journey while finding peace within your own.

Talk to Me:

"Archangel Uriel, guide me with wisdom and clarity as I care for my aging parents. Help me approach this time with understanding and peace. Thank you for your insight."

Archangel Zadkiel

On Aging Parents:

Forgiveness becomes vital in the care of aging parents. Old wounds and misunderstandings resurface, but this time also offers healing. I bring comfort to help you release resentment, replacing it with compassion. In forgiveness, you will find the freedom to connect with them fully.

Talk to Me:

"Archangel Zadkiel, help me forgive and heal old wounds with my parents. Bring comfort and compassion into our relationship. Thank you for your loving presence."

Archangel Metatron

On Aging Parents:

The care of parents is a sacred responsibility tied to your soul's growth. I help you see this experience as part of your divine path, guiding you to approach it with patience and love. Through this, you align with the higher wisdom of your soul's purpose.

Talk to Me:

"Archangel Metatron, guide me to see the divine purpose in caring for my parents. Help me grow spiritually through this sacred responsibility. Thank you for your insight."

Archangel Chamuel

On Aging Parents:

Caring for aging parents often awakens feelings of loss or abandonment. I bring emotional healing, helping you navigate the shifting roles with grace. Let me fill your heart with self-love and peace as you honor both your needs and theirs in this delicate dance of care.

LIFE THROUGH ANGEL EYES

Talk to Me:

"Archangel Chamuel, bring peace and emotional healing to this journey. Help me honor my parents with love while caring for myself. Thank you for your gentle guidance."

Archangel Samuel

On Aging Parents:

This stage often feels physically and emotionally exhausting. I help restore your vitality, guiding you to find rest and balance amidst caregiving. Together, we will create a rhythm that allows you to be present for your parents while nurturing your own well-being.

Talk to Me:

"Archangel Samuel, renew my energy and strength as I care for my parents. Help me find balance and vitality in this season of life. Thank you for your loving care."

Archangel Zachariel

On Aging Parents:

The challenges of caregiving can sometimes stir frustration or destructive tendencies. I help you find strength in these moments, guiding you to approach difficulties with patience. Lean into the resilience within you; it's stronger than you realize. Together, we'll turn hardship into growth.

Talk to Me:

"Archangel Zachariel, help me stay patient and strong in the face of challenges with my parents. Guide me to grow through this journey. Thank you for your unwavering support."

CH JODI M DEHN

Archangel Jophiel

On Aging Parents:

Even in difficult moments, beauty exists in caring for aging parents. I help you see the grace in their stories, the wisdom in their struggles, and the love that binds you. Let gratitude replace frustration, and joy will blossom even in the smallest moments.

Talk to Me:

"Archangel Jophiel, help me see the beauty and grace in this stage of my parents' lives. Fill me with gratitude for the love we share. Thank you for your light."

Archangel Laviah

On Aging Parents:

Dreams and intuition can provide guidance in caregiving. I help you tune into these subtle messages, uncovering insights that ease your path. Pay attention to the whispers of your heart and mind—they hold wisdom that transcends words.

Talk to Me:

"Archangel Laviah, guide my dreams and intuition as I navigate caring for my parents. Help me trust the wisdom within me. Thank you for your gentle guidance."

Archangel Sandalphon

On Aging Parents:

This journey requires balance, much like a harmonious melody. I help you stay grounded and steady, even amidst chaos. Together, we'll create a rhythm that honors your parents while keeping you connected to your own life's song.

Talk to Me:

"Archangel Sandalphon, ground me in peace and balance as I care for my parents. Help me find harmony in this journey. Thank you for your steadfast presence."

Archangel Jeremiel

On Aging Parents:

Caring for aging parents often invites reflection—on the past, present, and future. I help you find clarity, forgive where needed, and plan for moments of connection and love. This is a time of transformation for you and your family, and I will guide you through it.

Talk to Me:

"Archangel Jeremiel, help me reflect and find clarity in this journey. Guide me to forgive and plan for meaningful moments with my parents. Thank you for your wisdom."

Archangel Raguel

On Aging Parents:

Family dynamics can be challenging when caring for aging parents. I help bring harmony to disagreements and fairness to decisions, ensuring all voices are heard. Together, we'll create an atmosphere of understanding that supports your parents and strengthens family bonds.

Talk to Me:

"Archangel Raguel, guide me to foster harmony and understanding in my family. Help me navigate conflicts with fairness and compassion. Thank you for your loving support."

Archangel Haniel

On Aging Parents:

This is a time of emotional shifts, and I help you find balance amidst the change. Embrace your emotions without fear; they are part of this sacred process. Together, we'll cultivate harmony within your heart as you navigate this tender time with grace.

Talk to Me:

"Archangel Haniel, guide me to balance my emotions as I care for my parents. Help me approach this journey with grace and love. Thank you for your light."

ON HARMONY

Archangel Michael

On Harmony:

Harmony begins with courage—the courage to cut through confusion and protect what matters most. I help you create a foundation of stability by setting clear boundaries and removing fear and doubt. When you stand strong and resolute, peace can flourish in your relationships and within yourself. Harmony isn't the absence of conflict but the presence of balance in the face of challenges.

Talk to Me:

"Archangel Michael, lend me the strength to set boundaries and remove fear. Help me cultivate stability and balance so harmony can grow in my life. Thank you for your protection."

Archangel Gabriel

On Harmony:

Harmony is born in communication—words spoken with honesty and grace. I help you find the right words to soothe tensions and inspire connection. Whether in whispers or declarations, your voice can be the melody that brings balance and understanding to any situation. Trust in your ability to create peace through expression.

Talk to Me:

"Archangel Gabriel, guide my words to be kind and truthful, fostering harmony wherever I speak. Help me communicate with love and clarity. Thank you for your support."

CH JODI M DEHN

Archangel Raphael

On Harmony:

Healing and harmony go hand in hand. I mend the invisible wounds that disrupt balance in your heart and relationships. Let me soothe the discord within, so peace can radiate outward. Through healing—physical, emotional, and spiritual—you will rediscover the wholeness that brings harmony to all aspects of your life.

Talk to Me:

"Archangel Raphael, heal the wounds that keep me from harmony. Bring peace to my heart and relationships. Thank you for your gentle healing."

Archangel Uriel

On Harmony:

Harmony arises from wisdom. I bring clarity to confusion and illuminate the steps toward peace. Even in the darkest moments, my light guides you to understanding and resolution. Trust in the quiet wisdom within you, for it holds the key to uniting discordant elements into a seamless whole.

Talk to Me:

"Archangel Uriel, shine your light on my path and guide me to the wisdom that fosters harmony. Help me resolve conflicts with understanding. Thank you for your insight."

Archangel Zadkiel

On Harmony:

LIFE THROUGH ANGEL EYES

Forgiveness is the doorway to harmony. I help you release grudges and find compassion, even in challenging circumstances. Let go of the chains of resentment, and harmony will fill the space left behind. Through forgiveness, you not only heal others but find peace within yourself.

Talk to Me:

"Archangel Zadkiel, help me forgive and release resentment so harmony can take root in my life. Guide me toward compassion and peace. Thank you for your love."

Archangel Metatron

On Harmony:

Harmony aligns with your soul's higher purpose. I bring clarity to your path, helping you live in alignment with your truth. When you honor your divine calling, harmony naturally follows, connecting your inner world to the greater flow of the universe. Let me guide you toward this sacred balance.

Talk to Me:

"Archangel Metatron, align me with my soul's purpose so harmony may flow through my life. Help me honor my truth and bring peace to my journey. Thank you for your wisdom."

Archangel Chamuel

On Harmony:

I help you nurture harmony in your relationships, especially when emotions run high. Whether within a family, a partnership, or with yourself, love is the root of balance. Let me soothe your heart, restore your sense of self, and guide you toward deeper connections built on trust and understanding.

Talk to Me:

"Archangel Chamuel, bring harmony to my relationships and peace to my heart. Help me nurture love and understanding in all areas of my life. Thank you for your care."

Archangel Samuel

On Harmony:

Harmony requires vitality and balance. I bring restoration to your spirit and help you find moments of calm amidst life's chaos. Together, we'll create a rhythm of rest and renewal that allows harmony to thrive. When you are energized and centered, peace flows naturally into your life.

Talk to Me:

"Archangel Samuel, renew my energy and guide me toward balance and peace. Help me create harmony in my daily life. Thank you for your strength."

Archangel Zachariel

On Harmony:

When conflict arises, strength and discernment are needed to restore balance. I help you channel your power constructively, turning discord into an opportunity for growth. Harmony isn't a passive state; it's something you build with intention and resilience. Together, we'll create stability out of chaos.

Talk to Me:

LIFE THROUGH ANGEL EYES

"Archangel Zachariel, guide me to use my strength to create harmony in challenging situations. Help me turn discord into peace. Thank you for your guidance."

Archangel Jophiel

On Harmony:

Harmony begins when you see the beauty in all things. I help you find gratitude even in difficult times and recognize the goodness around you. When your perspective shifts, harmony blooms naturally, bringing balance to your inner world and radiating outward into your life.

Talk to Me:

"Archangel Jophiel, open my eyes to the beauty and goodness that foster harmony. Help me approach life with gratitude and joy. Thank you for your light."

Archangel Laviah

On Harmony:

Dreams hold the secrets to harmony. In the quiet of sleep, I guide your subconscious toward balance, offering insights and solutions that elude you in waking hours. Trust the gentle whispers of your dreams—they carry the wisdom you need to create peace within and around you.

Talk to Me:

"Archangel Laviah, guide my dreams to reveal the path to harmony. Help me trust the wisdom of my subconscious. Thank you for your gentle presence."

Archangel Sandalphon

On Harmony:

Harmony, like music, requires rhythm and flow. I help you ground yourself in the present, balancing your energy so life feels like a beautiful symphony. Let me attune your spirit to the natural cadence of peace, ensuring every note of your journey resonates with love and balance.

Talk to Me:

"Archangel Sandalphon, guide me to find harmony in the rhythm of my life. Help me stay grounded and connected to peace. Thank you for your steady support."

Archangel Jeremiel

On Harmony:

Reflection brings harmony. I help you look back with clarity and forward with hope, finding balance between where you've been and where you're going. Together, we'll create a vision of peace and fulfillment, ensuring your past, present, and future align harmoniously.

Talk to Me:

"Archangel Jeremiel, guide my reflections and help me create harmony between my past and future. Thank you for your clarity and insight."

Archangel Raguel

On Harmony:

LIFE THROUGH ANGEL EYES

Harmony thrives in fairness and mutual respect. I help mediate conflicts and bring understanding where it's needed most. Whether in relationships or decisions, I ensure balance and equity prevail, creating the foundation for lasting peace.

Talk to Me:

"Archangel Raguel, bring fairness and understanding to my interactions. Help me create harmony through mutual respect and balance. Thank you for your love."

Archangel Haniel

On Harmony:

Harmony comes from emotional balance. I help you embrace your feelings without letting them overwhelm you, finding peace even in life's storms. Trust the ebb and flow of your emotions—they're part of the beautiful tapestry of your life. Together, we'll weave harmony into your soul.

Talk to Me:

"Archangel Haniel, guide me to balance my emotions and create harmony within myself. Help me embrace peace in every moment. Thank you for your gentle care."

ON MENOPAUSE

Archangel Michael

On Menopause:

Menopause is a powerful shift, not a loss. I stand beside you as you release fear and face the unknown with courage. This is not an end but a transformation, where you reclaim strength and redefine your boundaries. Let me protect your energy as you step into this new chapter of wisdom and empowerment.

Talk to Me:

"Archangel Michael, help me release fear and embrace this transition with courage and strength. Protect my spirit and guide me toward empowerment. Thank you for your unwavering support."

Archangel Gabriel

On Menopause:

Your body's transformation may test your communication with yourself and others. I help you express your needs, feelings, and concerns with grace. Menopause is not something to hide but to honor—let your voice be clear, your truth spoken, and your joy reclaimed. Embrace the changes as a story of growth.

Talk to Me:

"Archangel Gabriel, help me communicate my needs and emotions clearly during this time. Guide me to find joy and honor my journey. Thank you for your guidance."

Archangel Raphael

LIFE THROUGH ANGEL EYES

On Menopause:

Menopause requires healing—not just physical but emotional and spiritual. I bring relief to discomfort, soothing your mind and body as they adjust. Let me show you that this change carries a gift: deeper self-awareness, renewal, and the chance to honor your body's wisdom. Healing begins with acceptance.

Talk to Me:

"Archangel Raphael, heal my body and bring me comfort as I navigate menopause. Help me embrace the gifts of this transformation. Thank you for your healing presence."

Archangel Uriel

On Menopause:

Menopause brings moments of despair, confusion, and fear. I offer you wisdom and light to see beyond the discomfort. Let this phase awaken new ideas and inspire you to redefine your purpose. In stillness, you'll find peace and a tranquil understanding of the woman you are becoming.

Talk to Me:

"Archangel Uriel, illuminate this path of change with your wisdom. Help me find peace, purpose, and understanding during this time. Thank you for your guidance."

Archangel Zadkiel

On Menopause:

Menopause asks for forgiveness—of your body, of yourself, and of expectations you've held for years. Release guilt and accept that change is natural. I bring calm, comfort, and discernment as you navigate emotional shifts. Let me guide you to see this time as sacred, freeing you to embrace new wisdom.

Talk to Me:

"Archangel Zadkiel, help me release guilt and find calm during menopause. Show me the wisdom in this transition and bring me comfort. Thank you for your love."

Archangel Metatron

On Menopause:

Menopause is an initiation into higher wisdom. Your body shifts, but your spirit rises, awakening deeper truths about yourself and your life's purpose. I help you see beyond discomfort to the enlightenment that awaits. Trust this process—you are stepping into a phase of empowerment and clarity.

Talk to Me:

"Archangel Metatron, guide me to the wisdom and enlightenment that menopause brings. Help me embrace this transformation as a sacred initiation. Thank you for your light."

Archangel Chamuel

On Menopause:

This is a time to reconnect with your inner child and nurture self-love. The changes can bring feelings of loss, abandonment, or confusion, but I help you embrace peace and emotional healing. Menopause is a chance to care for yourself deeply and rediscover who you are at your core.

LIFE THROUGH ANGEL EYES

Talk to Me:

"Archangel Chamuel, help me find peace and self-love during this time of change. Heal my heart and reconnect me to my true self. Thank you for your gentle care."

Archangel Samuel

On Menopause:

Fatigue and restlessness often accompany menopause. I bring you the vitality to move through this phase with strength and grace. Sleep may elude you, but I help restore balance to your energy. Know that this is temporary—you are renewing, resetting, and stepping into a season of self-discovery.

Talk to Me:

"Archangel Samuel, restore my energy and bring me peaceful rest. Help me move through this transition with vitality and grace. Thank you for your strength."

Archangel Zachariel

On Menopause:

You may feel at odds with your body, as if it's no longer yours. I help you find strength to overcome destructive thoughts and fears. Menopause is not a battle; it's a calling to transform. I guide you to face this process with acceptance and unwavering confidence in your resilience.

Talk to Me:

"Archangel Zachariel, give me strength to overcome the challenges of menopause. Help me embrace my body and this change with confidence. Thank you for your courage."

Archangel Jophiel

On Menopause:

Your body's changes are not to be despised but celebrated for their beauty and wisdom. I help you see yourself through eyes of gratitude and grace, shifting away from unhealthy thoughts or self-criticism. Menopause is a chance to focus on your goals and redefine what makes life beautiful to you.

Talk to Me:

"Archangel Jophiel, help me see the beauty in this time of change. Inspire gratitude, grace, and renewed focus on what brings me joy. Thank you for your light."

Archangel Laviah

On Menopause:

Your dreams during menopause may carry profound revelations. I guide your subconscious to reveal what you need—wisdom, release, or inspiration. This transition can be confusing, but your intuition will ground you. Allow your dreams to speak, for they hold answers to this sacred unfolding.

Talk to Me:

"Archangel Laviah, guide my dreams to reveal wisdom and clarity during menopause. Help me trust the messages within. Thank you for your presence."

LIFE THROUGH ANGEL EYES

Archangel Sandalphon

On Menopause:

Menopause can feel ungrounded, like the rhythm of life has shifted. I help you reconnect to the earth's steady energy and find peace in your body. Music, movement, and nature are tools I offer to help you rediscover harmony as you transition into this new phase of being.

Talk to Me:

"Archangel Sandalphon, help me ground my energy and find peace in this transition. Guide me through music and movement toward balance. Thank you for your care."

Archangel Jeremiel

On Menopause:

Menopause is a time for reflection—on where you've been, who you are, and where you're going. I help you review your life with compassion and hope, guiding you to plan for a future aligned with your heart's desires. This is not an ending; it's a chance for renewal and clarity.

Talk to Me:

"Archangel Jeremiel, guide me in reflecting on my life with love and hope. Help me see this transition as a time for renewal. Thank you for your insight."

Archangel Raguel

On Menopause:

Harmony within relationships can feel strained during menopause. I help you restore fairness and balance, ensuring your voice is heard and understood. Be patient with yourself and others during this process. Together, we'll create peace, clarity, and stronger connections as you step into this new chapter.

Talk to Me:

"Archangel Raguel, bring harmony to my relationships and help me express my needs during menopause. Guide me to fairness and peace. Thank you for your support."

Archangel Haniel

On Menopause:

Your emotions may feel like a tidal wave, but I help you ride them with grace. I bring balance and harmony to your spirit, helping you honor the wisdom this phase offers. Menopause is a transition into emotional freedom, where you are no longer defined by old limitations.

Talk to Me:

"Archangel Haniel, guide me to emotional balance and help me embrace the freedom menopause brings. Let me flow with grace through this transition. Thank you for your care."

ON WAKING

Archangel Michael

On Waking:

Each morning is a new beginning—a chance to let go of fears carried through the night and stand strong in your purpose. I guard your rest, and as you wake, I empower you with courage. Let me fortify you with clear focus, dispelling any lingering doubts from the night.

Talk to Me:

"Archangel Michael, fill me with courage and strength as I awaken. Release my fears and guide me to embrace this day with confidence. Thank you for your protection."

Archangel Gabriel

On Waking:

Morning is the perfect time to reconnect with your voice. As you wake, allow your thoughts to flow freely—dreams, ideas, truths yet spoken. I help you clear away foggy feelings and embrace the clarity of a new day. Start fresh, speak from your heart, and welcome joy.

Talk to Me:

"Archangel Gabriel, help me awaken with clarity and joy. Guide me to speak my truth and honor my thoughts as I begin this day. Thank you for your light."

Archangel Raphael

On Waking:

As you rise, your body recalibrates, seeking balance after rest. I infuse you with healing energy, helping you move past any discomfort or fatigue. Let the gift of a new day renew your mind and spirit. I bring comfort so you can rise feeling whole and ready.

Talk to Me:

"Archangel Raphael, fill me with healing energy as I wake. Bring comfort to my body and clarity to my mind. Thank you for your gentle touch."

Archangel Uriel

On Waking:

Waking is an invitation to wisdom. The quiet moments between sleep and the day hold answers to your worries and ideas for your journey. I help you listen for clarity, turning your thoughts from fear to peace. Let me bring you light as you step into the new day.

Talk to Me:

"Archangel Uriel, awaken my mind with clarity and wisdom. Help me find peace in the quiet moments of morning. Thank you for your insight."

Archangel Zadkiel

On Waking:

Morning is a time to release heavy emotions from yesterday. I wrap you in calm and comfort, helping you forgive yourself and others. Let go of guilt or doubt lingering in your heart. Each morning is a chance to move forward with wisdom and a lighter spirit.

Talk to Me:

"Archangel Zadkiel, fill me with calm as I wake. Help me release burdens and embrace forgiveness. Thank you for your comforting presence."

Archangel Metatron

On Waking:

With each waking, your purpose calls you. The first thoughts of the day hold opportunities for clarity and self-discovery. I help you align your mind and energy with your higher purpose, guiding you to honor your path. Let today awaken a deeper connection to your true self.

Talk to Me:

"Archangel Metatron, guide me to align with my purpose as I wake. Help me see the truth of my path with clarity. Thank you for your enlightenment."

Archangel Chamuel

On Waking:

As you wake, notice how your heart feels. Is there peace? Or do you need to nurture it today? I help you reconnect with love—for yourself, for others, for life. The morning brings emotional renewal, an invitation to begin the day with compassion and gentle understanding.

Talk to Me:

"Archangel Chamuel, guide me to wake with a loving and peaceful heart. Help me embrace emotional healing today. Thank you for your gentle care."

CH JODI M DEHN

Archangel Samuel

On Waking:

Waking after a restless night can feel heavy, but I restore your energy. Let me help you find vitality in the morning light and breathe life into your tired soul. This day is a gift—I help you move through it with renewed strength and focus.

Talk to Me:

"Archangel Samuel, renew my energy as I wake. Fill me with strength and focus for the day ahead. Thank you for your support."

Archangel Zachariel

On Waking:

Waking is an opportunity to face challenges with strength. If problems wait for you in the day, let me stand by you. I help you rise with courage, banishing destructive thoughts or hesitation. You are strong enough to tackle anything that lies ahead—step forward with confidence.

Talk to Me:

"Archangel Zachariel, awaken my strength and courage for the day. Help me face my challenges with confidence. Thank you for standing with me."

Archangel Jophiel

On Waking:

Each morning is an opportunity to see beauty in life. I help you wake with gratitude and joy, clearing away unhealthy thoughts that cloud your vision. Whether big or small, blessings surround you. Open

LIFE THROUGH ANGEL EYES

your heart and begin the day with appreciation for the beauty within and around you.

Talk to Me:

"Archangel Jophiel, awaken my heart with gratitude and joy. Help me see the beauty of this new day. Thank you for your inspiration."

Archangel Laviah

On Waking:

Waking after dreaming brings a bridge between worlds. Your dreams whisper messages—wisdom, comfort, or signs for your path. I help you recall what matters and trust your intuition. The quiet clarity of morning carries truth from your subconscious. Honor it and let it guide you.

Talk to Me:

"Archangel Laviah, help me remember and trust the wisdom in my dreams. Awaken my intuition as I begin this day. Thank you for your insight."

Archangel Sandalphon

On Waking:

Morning is a rhythm—a soft return to life's song. I help you reconnect with grounded energy as you wake. Music, movement, and quiet reflection will set the tone for your day. Let me guide you to rise with balance and flow, steady and sure in your steps forward.

Talk to Me:

"Archangel Sandalphon, help me wake with balance and harmony. Guide my steps as I reconnect with life's rhythm today. Thank you for your grounding presence."

Archangel Jeremiel

On Waking:

Morning is a natural review—a pause to reflect before moving forward. I help you see what matters most today, offering clarity for your intentions. Each new morning is a chance for growth, change, and hope. Let me guide you to step into this day with renewed purpose.

Talk to Me:

"Archangel Jeremiel, help me wake with clarity and hope. Guide my thoughts as I set intentions for today. Thank you for your insight."

Archangel Raguel

On Waking:

Waking renews your connection to the world and relationships. I help you start fresh with fairness and harmony in your heart. Let go of misunderstandings or conflicts from yesterday and approach the day with a balanced mind, ready to restore peace and connection with yourself and others.

Talk to Me:

"Archangel Raguel, awaken harmony within me as I begin this day. Guide me to approach relationships with fairness and peace. Thank you for your balance."

Archangel Haniel

LIFE THROUGH ANGEL EYES

On Waking:

The morning is sacred—a bridge between rest and action. I help you wake with emotional balance and a clear connection to your intuition. Trust the subtle feelings that arise as you step into your day. Your spirit is aligning with harmony and purpose—let it guide you.

Talk to Me:

"Archangel Haniel, help me wake with balance and trust in my intuition. Guide my emotions and spirit as I step into today. Thank you for your grace."

ON JOB LOSS

Archangel Michael

On Job Loss:

Job loss can leave you feeling vulnerable, but I remind you that this is not the end—it's a shift. I protect your energy, cutting cords of fear and self-doubt. Stand firm as I guide you to see your worth beyond a role or title. You are resilient and capable of rising stronger.

Talk to Me:

"Archangel Michael, protect me as I navigate this change. Help me release fear and step into new opportunities with confidence. Thank you for your strength and courage."

Archangel Gabriel

On Job Loss:

Losing a job can silence your voice and stifle creativity, but I see this as an opportunity for renewal. I guide you to express your thoughts, ideas, and desires clearly, helping you rewrite your story. Let joy return as you discover a fresh path, full of new inspiration.

Talk to Me:

"Archangel Gabriel, guide me to express myself and find clarity in this transition. Help me discover a new purpose where my gifts can shine. Thank you for your support."

Archangel Raphael

On Job Loss:

LIFE THROUGH ANGEL EYES

Job loss weighs heavily on the body and mind, bringing stress and emotional exhaustion. I soothe these wounds and bring healing energy to restore your strength. Take a deep breath, rest, and let me help you rebuild—mentally, physically, and emotionally—so you move forward renewed and ready.

Talk to Me:

"Archangel Raphael, bring healing to my mind, body, and spirit as I navigate this change. Restore my energy and help me move forward with hope. Thank you for your care."

Archangel Uriel

On Job Loss:

When despair clouds your thoughts and fear paralyzes your decisions, I bring wisdom and light. Let me help you see this challenge as a doorway to new ideas. Ground yourself, breathe, and allow fresh inspiration to flow. In every ending, I help you uncover the seeds of a new beginning.

Talk to Me:

"Archangel Uriel, guide me out of fear and despair. Fill me with wisdom and clarity to find new opportunities. Thank you for showing me the light ahead."

Archangel Zadkiel

On Job Loss:

This is a time to forgive yourself and others. Release guilt, anger, or blame, and allow calm to enter your heart. I help you discern the lessons hidden in this experience, transforming pain into wisdom. From a place of peace, new opportunities can flourish.

Talk to Me:

"Archangel Zadkiel, help me release guilt and embrace forgiveness. Guide me to see the wisdom in this challenge and step forward with clarity. Thank you for your peace."

Archangel Metatron

On Job Loss:

Job loss can shatter confidence, especially when purpose feels unclear. I help you realign with your soul's mission. You are not defined by a title but by the light you bring to the world. I'll guide you to opportunities that reflect your highest potential and true purpose.

Talk to Me:

"Archangel Metatron, realign me with my soul's purpose and guide me toward opportunities that uplift and fulfill me. Thank you for your wisdom and clarity."

Archangel Chamuel

On Job Loss:

The loss of a job can feel like rejection or abandonment, leaving a void in your heart. I help you reconnect with self-love and inner peace. From this place of emotional healing, you'll rediscover your value and attract work that supports your well-being and happiness.

Talk to Me:

"Archangel Chamuel, heal my heart and remind me of my worth. Guide me to opportunities that bring joy, peace, and fulfillment. Thank you for your love."

LIFE THROUGH ANGEL EYES

Archangel Samuel

On Job Loss:

Losing a job disrupts your energy and routines, leaving you tired and adrift. I help you restore your vitality, reestablish healthy habits, and embrace restful sleep. With renewed strength, you'll gain the motivation needed to build a new path and step confidently into the future.

Talk to Me:

"Archangel Samuel, restore my energy and help me find motivation as I rebuild. Guide me to balance my rest and work. Thank you for your support."

Archangel Zachariel

On Job Loss:

Job loss can trigger destructive thoughts: anger, self-blame, or hopelessness. I help you break these patterns, grounding you in strength and clarity. Lean on me as you face challenges head-on. You are stronger than this moment, and new opportunities will emerge when you choose forward momentum.

Talk to Me:

"Archangel Zachariel, help me break free from destructive thoughts. Strengthen me to rise above challenges and see opportunities. Thank you for your courage and clarity."

Archangel Jophiel

On Job Loss:

Job loss can cloud your mind with negativity, but I show you the beauty in every stage of life. This transition is a chance to redefine your goals and align them with your heart. Be grateful for the lessons learned and trust that a brighter future awaits.

Talk to Me:

"Archangel Jophiel, clear my mind of negativity and help me see the beauty in this transition. Guide me to set goals that bring joy. Thank you for your light."

Archangel Laviah

On Job Loss:

In uncertain times, I help you connect with your dreams and intuition. This is a moment to reflect deeply on what you truly desire. I'll guide you through quiet stillness, showing you new directions and possibilities revealed through your inner wisdom. Trust what you feel.

Talk to Me:

"Archangel Laviah, guide me to quiet reflection and deep understanding of my purpose. Show me the opportunities waiting for me. Thank you for your guidance."

Archangel Sandalphon

On Job Loss:

I remind you to stay grounded when emotions run high. Music, nature, or meditation can center your energy, helping you process grief or frustration. By reconnecting with the rhythm of life, you'll rediscover peace and begin to trust that better opportunities are already unfolding.

LIFE THROUGH ANGEL EYES

Talk to Me:

"Archangel Sandalphon, help me ground my emotions and find peace in this transition. Guide me to opportunities that align with my soul. Thank you for your harmony."

Archangel Jeremiel

On Job Loss:

This is a time of reflection, not regret. I help you review your journey and learn from every experience. Where can you grow? What do you truly desire? Allow me to guide you as you plan for positive change, turning this ending into a doorway for new possibilities.

Talk to Me:

"Archangel Jeremiel, help me reflect on this change with clarity. Guide me to create a future filled with purpose and hope. Thank you for your insight."

Archangel Raguel

On Job Loss:

Job loss can strain relationships or create feelings of injustice. I help you restore balance and peace with yourself and others. Trust that harmony will return, and new paths will open where you can thrive. Let me guide you toward resolutions and renewed hope.

Talk to Me:

"Archangel Raguel, help me release feelings of unfairness and restore peace. Guide me toward opportunities where I can grow. Thank you for your support."

Archangel Haniel

CH JODI M DEHN

On Job Loss:

Losing a job can feel like losing balance, but I help you reconnect to your emotional center. Just as the moon's cycles bring change, this phase holds purpose. Allow yourself to grieve, then rise with grace and trust. You will find harmony and fulfillment once again.

Talk to Me:

"Archangel Haniel, guide me to embrace this transition with grace. Help me find emotional balance and trust in the opportunities ahead. Thank you for your light."

ON PEACE

Archangel Michael

On Peace:

Peace in your soul comes when you are free—free from fear, doubt, and the chains of old battles. I help you stand strong, knowing that you are protected and secure. It's not about a quiet world but a fearless heart that holds steady amidst life's storms. Let me cut away the noise and chaos, replacing it with clarity and courage.

Talk to Me:

"Archangel Michael, shield me from fear and inner turmoil. Cut away what keeps me from peace, and fill me with strength and unwavering calm. Thank you for your protection."

Archangel Gabriel

On Peace:

Peace is the voice of truth within you. It sings softly when you are aligned with your purpose and free to express yourself without shame or guilt. I guide you to communicate honestly with yourself and others, clearing misunderstandings and embracing joy. When your words and heart are in harmony, peace flows naturally.

Talk to Me:

"Archangel Gabriel, help me find peace in honest communication and joyful expression. Let my voice reflect the truth of my soul. Thank you for your guidance."

Archangel Raphael

On Peace:

True peace begins with healing—healing your body, mind, and spirit. When wounds go unaddressed, they ripple through your soul, stealing calm. I pour soothing energy into your being, helping you release pain and embrace wholeness. A healed soul radiates peace, allowing you to breathe deeply and live freely.

Talk to Me:

"Archangel Raphael, heal my wounds and restore balance to my body and spirit. Guide me to peace through complete healing. Thank you for your care."

Archangel Uriel

On Peace:

Peace is found in the light of wisdom when fear no longer clouds your vision. I help you see the truth, even in dark times. Tranquility comes from knowing that each moment, even the painful ones, holds purpose. I bring understanding to ease despair and replace it with calm certainty.

Talk to Me:

"Archangel Uriel, shine your light on my fears and doubts. Fill me with wisdom and help me trust in the path ahead. Thank you for your guidance."

Archangel Zadkiel

On Peace:

Forgiveness is the key to peace within your soul. Anger, guilt, or resentment erode the calm you seek. I help you release these burdens, offering compassion to yourself and others. As you forgive, peace unfolds like a gentle wave, bringing comfort, clarity, and calm to your inner world.

Talk to Me:

"Archangel Zadkiel, guide me to release all that disrupts my peace. Help me forgive, find comfort, and embrace calm. Thank you for your light."

Archangel Metatron

On Peace:

Peace comes from living aligned with your divine purpose. When you drift from your truth, restlessness grows. I help you reconnect with your higher self, elevating your awareness. You'll find peace in knowing you are walking a path uniquely designed for your soul's growth and enlightenment.

Talk to Me:

"Archangel Metatron, align me with my higher purpose. Help me find peace by reconnecting with the truth of who I am. Thank you for your clarity."

Archangel Chamuel

On Peace:

Peace begins in the heart. When love replaces self-doubt and emotional wounds are healed, harmony follows. I guide you to nurture your inner child, embracing self-love and compassion. True peace flows when you stop searching for it outside yourself and find it within.

Talk to Me:

"Archangel Chamuel, heal my heart and guide me to peace through self-love and compassion. Help me release pain and embrace harmony. Thank you for your love."

Archangel Samuel

On Peace:

Restlessness steals your peace, leaving you physically and emotionally drained. I help you restore balance, guiding you to restful sleep and renewed vitality. When your body is nurtured and your energy is clear, the stillness of peace settles into your soul like morning light breaking through the fog.

Talk to Me:

"Archangel Samuel, bring rest and balance to my body and mind. Help me reclaim the peace that comes with renewed energy. Thank you for your care."

Archangel Zachariel

On Peace:

When destructive thoughts and turmoil disrupt your soul, peace feels far away. I help you confront these challenges with strength, replacing chaos with calm resolve. Peace isn't about avoiding problems but mastering your response to them, knowing you are strong enough to weather any storm.

Talk to Me:

LIFE THROUGH ANGEL EYES

"Archangel Zachariel, guide me to overcome inner conflict and find strength in calm. Help me embrace peace as I face life's challenges. Thank you for your courage."

Archangel Jophiel

On Peace:

Peace comes when you shift your perspective. Instead of focusing on what's wrong, I help you see beauty in the present moment. Gratitude and wonder bring peace, turning even the ordinary into a source of joy. Let me help you clear negative thoughts and embrace life's blessings.

Talk to Me:

"Archangel Jophiel, clear my mind and show me the beauty in my life. Help me find peace through gratitude and joy. Thank you for your light."

Archangel Laviah

On Peace:

Peace resides in the quiet depths of your soul, where intuition speaks and dreams reveal truth. I guide you to this stillness, helping you trust your inner wisdom. Let go of surface distractions and listen. Peace is waiting, like a gentle whisper beneath the noise of life.

Talk to Me:

"Archangel Laviah, guide me to the quiet within. Help me hear the truth of my soul and embrace the peace waiting there. Thank you for your insight."

Archangel Sandalphon

CH JODI M DEHN

On Peace:

Peace is groundedness, a harmony between earth and spirit. Music, movement, and nature are tools I use to restore your balance. When you feel scattered or disconnected, I guide you to plant your feet, breathe deeply, and reconnect with the gentle rhythm of life.

Talk to Me:

"Archangel Sandalphon, ground me in peace. Help me find balance through music, nature, and stillness. Thank you for your harmony."

Archangel Jeremiel

On Peace:

Peace is found through reflection. When you review your life without judgment, seeing both the challenges and the blessings, your soul settles. I help you release regrets and plan for a more peaceful, purposeful future. True peace comes when you embrace where you've been and where you're going.

Talk to Me:

"Archangel Jeremiel, help me reflect with clarity and peace. Guide me to release regrets and embrace the path forward. Thank you for your insight."

Archangel Raguel

On Peace:

Peace in your soul begins with harmony in your relationships. I help you heal misunderstandings, dissolve resentment, and restore balance. When love and compassion guide your connections, the unrest within fades. Let me bring unity where there is conflict, and calm where there is tension.

Talk to Me:

"Archangel Raguel, bring harmony to my relationships and peace to my soul. Help me release resentment and embrace love. Thank you for your support."

Archangel Haniel

On Peace:

Peace is the grace of balance, like the moon gently guiding the tides. I help you embrace life's cycles without resistance. Even in moments of uncertainty or emotional turmoil, I guide you back to harmony. Peace flows when you surrender and trust the rhythm of your soul's journey.

Talk to Me:

"Archangel Haniel, guide me to embrace life's cycles with grace. Help me find peace in trust and balance. Thank you for your light."

ON ABUNDANCE

Archangel Michael

On Abundance:

Abundance is a life lived with strength, courage, and freedom from fear. It's the overflowing confidence that you are protected and guided at every step. I help you release scarcity thinking—those doubts and fears that whisper, "Not enough." True abundance begins when you trust in your worth and in the endless support of the universe. Stand tall, unshaken, and watch abundance flow to meet your courage.

Talk to Me:

"Archangel Michael, cut through my fears of scarcity and doubt. Help me stand strong and open to the abundance meant for me. Thank you for your protection."

Archangel Gabriel

On Abundance:

Abundance blooms when you allow your creativity and joy to flow unhindered. It's not just material wealth but a richness of expression, communication, and purpose. I help you clear blocks to inspiration and find joy in sharing your gifts. When your voice and talents shine, abundance follows naturally.

Talk to Me:

"Archangel Gabriel, inspire me to express my gifts and talents freely. Help me create joy and abundance in all I do. Thank you for your guidance."

LIFE THROUGH ANGEL EYES

Archangel Raphael

On Abundance:

Abundance begins with health—vitality of the body, mind, and spirit. Without wellness, life feels restricted, no matter the external riches. I help you heal, replenish, and open yourself to the fullness of life. True abundance comes when your energy flows freely, and your body thrives in harmony.

Talk to Me:

"Archangel Raphael, heal me in body and soul so I may embrace the fullness of life. Guide me to health, joy, and boundless abundance. Thank you for your care."

Archangel Uriel

On Abundance:

Abundance thrives where wisdom and faith replace fear. It's trusting that life provides what you need, even when the path ahead feels unclear. I light up new ideas, solutions, and opportunities where others see only obstacles. Open your mind and heart to my guidance, and abundance will follow.

Talk to Me:

"Archangel Uriel, shine your light on my path and replace my fears with trust. Help me see the abundance and opportunities before me. Thank you for your wisdom."

Archangel Zadkiel

On Abundance:

Forgiveness opens the flow of abundance. Anger, guilt, or regret creates blockages that keep abundance at bay. I help you release these emotional chains so your soul can receive freely. True abundance arrives when your heart is light, open, and ready to accept all the universe offers.

Talk to Me:

"Archangel Zadkiel, help me forgive and release what weighs me down. Open my heart to receive the abundance that is meant for me. Thank you for your light."

Archangel Metatron

On Abundance:

Abundance comes when you align with your soul's higher purpose. When your actions and goals reflect who you truly are, the universe responds with limitless support. I guide you to recognize your worth, embrace your unique gifts, and step boldly onto the path of your divine blueprint.

Talk to Me:

"Archangel Metatron, help me align with my divine purpose and clear the way for abundance to flow. Thank you for your guidance and clarity."

Archangel Chamuel

On Abundance:

Abundance begins with love—love for yourself, others, and life. When you nurture your inner child and heal emotional wounds, you open yourself to life's limitless gifts. I help you clear feelings of unworthiness and replace them with self-love and peace. Love attracts abundance in all forms.

Talk to Me:

"Archangel Chamuel, guide me to embrace self-love and heal emotional blocks. Help me welcome the abundance I deserve. Thank you for your peace."

Archangel Samuel

On Abundance:

True abundance requires energy—physical, emotional, and spiritual. When exhaustion drains you, abundance feels unreachable. I guide you to rest, recharge, and regain vitality. With a renewed spirit and a clear path forward, abundance flows, unrestricted and limitless, into all areas of your life.

Talk to Me:

"Archangel Samuel, renew my energy and guide me to balance. Help me open my life to the flow of true abundance. Thank you for your strength."

Archangel Zachariel

On Abundance:

Abundance is strength—it is the ability to face life's challenges with resilience and courage. Where others see only limitations, I help you uncover opportunities. I guide you to conquer destructive habits and reclaim your power, knowing that you are capable of achieving all you need and more.

Talk to Me:

"Archangel Zachariel, help me overcome limitations and embrace my strength. Guide me to claim the abundance waiting for me. Thank you for your support."

Archangel Jophiel

On Abundance:

Abundance comes when you shift your perspective. It's seeing beauty, opportunity, and blessings where others see only lack. I clear away negativity and help you recognize the gifts already around you. Gratitude turns what you have into enough—and enough becomes overflow.

Talk to Me:

"Archangel Jophiel, open my eyes to the beauty and blessings in my life. Help me embrace abundance with gratitude and joy. Thank you for your light."

Archangel Laviah

On Abundance:

Abundance flows when you trust your intuition and dream without limits. I guide you to listen to your inner wisdom, showing you opportunities that align with your soul. When you act on what feels true and inspired, abundance appears like a dream realized in the waking world.

Talk to Me:

"Archangel Laviah, help me trust my intuition and see the path to abundance clearly. Guide me to fulfill my soul's dreams. Thank you for your insight."

LIFE THROUGH ANGEL EYES

Archangel Sandalphon

On Abundance:

Abundance is harmony—it's being grounded while reaching for the divine. I help you balance your energy, using music, movement, and nature to bring you back to center. When your spirit is calm and rooted, abundance flows effortlessly, connecting heaven's gifts with your earthly life.

Talk to Me:

"Archangel Sandalphon, ground me in harmony and open the flow of abundance into my life. Help me find peace and balance. Thank you for your grace."

Archangel Jeremiel

On Abundance:

Abundance comes when you reflect on where you've been and where you're going. By learning from the past and planning for a better future, you clear the path for life's blessings to flow. I help you release regrets, set intentions, and prepare to receive all that you're ready for.

Talk to Me:

"Archangel Jeremiel, guide me to reflect and plan for an abundant future. Help me release what holds me back and embrace new possibilities. Thank you for your insight."

Archangel Raguel

On Abundance:

Harmony in your relationships opens the doors to abundance. When misunderstandings, resentments, or conflicts cloud your life, you block the flow of blessings. I help restore balance, strengthening connections so that peace and prosperity can enter. Abundance thrives where love and understanding are present.

Talk to Me:

"Archangel Raguel, bring harmony to my relationships and clear the way for abundance to flow. Help me embrace connection and peace. Thank you for your love."

Archangel Haniel

On Abundance:

Abundance aligns with balance and grace—moving with life's cycles instead of resisting them. I help you trust that you are always provided for, even in times of change. When you honor the flow of life, you create space for abundance to bloom naturally and beautifully.

Talk to Me:

"Archangel Haniel, guide me to trust life's cycles and open my heart to receive abundance with grace. Thank you for your wisdom."

ON GRATITUDE

Archangel Michael

On Gratitude:

Gratitude is your shield and sword against fear. When you recognize the good in your life, however small, you disarm the voices that tell you you're lacking. I help you stand in your power and see how far you've come, anchoring your spirit in strength. Gratitude fuels courage, and courage opens doors.

Talk to Me:

"Archangel Michael, help me stand tall in gratitude and see my life through the lens of strength. Protect my spirit from doubt and fear. Thank you for your guidance."

Archangel Gabriel

On Gratitude:

Gratitude is a melody that harmonizes your soul. When you speak words of appreciation, even for life's simplest blessings, you tune yourself to joy. I help you communicate gratitude outwardly, sharing light with others. A grateful voice inspires and uplifts, rippling into a chorus of positivity.

Talk to Me:

"Archangel Gabriel, help me express gratitude with clarity and joy. Let my words become a blessing to myself and others. Thank you for your inspiration."

Archangel Raphael

CH JODI M DEHN

On Gratitude:

Gratitude is medicine for the heart and body. When you focus on what you appreciate, your energy calms, your mind clears, and healing begins. I help you find the blessings in difficult moments, showing you that gratitude nourishes both the physical and emotional self.

Talk to Me:

"Archangel Raphael, guide me to see the healing power of gratitude. Help me find peace and renewal in appreciating my journey. Thank you for your care."

Archangel Uriel

On Gratitude:

Gratitude shifts your perspective from fear to faith. I help you see how each challenge, mistake, or loss has brought you wisdom. Gratitude doesn't erase hardship, but it reveals its purpose. From this new understanding, you'll find peace, new ideas, and light where there was darkness.

Talk to Me:

"Archangel Uriel, help me uncover the lessons in my experiences and guide me to gratitude for all they've taught me. Thank you for your wisdom."

Archangel Zadkiel

On Gratitude:

Gratitude is a gateway to forgiveness and inner calm. It softens anger, eases anxiety, and shifts you away from "what is lacking" to "what is here." I help you appreciate others' efforts, see beauty in yourself, and free yourself from lingering resentments that block joy.

Talk to Me:

"Archangel Zadkiel, help me embrace gratitude to release what weighs me down. Fill me with appreciation for the blessings I have. Thank you for your peace."

Archangel Metatron

On Gratitude:

Gratitude elevates your vibration. It aligns you with divine energy, helping you see your life's path more clearly. I guide you to honor the small and big miracles in your journey and connect to your higher purpose. Gratitude awakens enlightenment, showing you the endless possibilities before you.

Talk to Me:

"Archangel Metatron, help me see the miracles in my life and align with gratitude. Elevate my energy and guide me toward my purpose. Thank you for your light."

Archangel Chamuel

On Gratitude:

Gratitude brings peace to the heart. When you feel unloved or unseen, it's easy to focus on what's missing. I guide you to find comfort in what is present—your strengths, relationships, and moments of quiet joy. Gratitude heals the wounds of abandonment and brings deep emotional restoration.

Talk to Me:

"Archangel Chamuel, help me find peace in gratitude. Heal my heart and show me the love and blessings already around me. Thank you for your comfort."

Archangel Samuel

On Gratitude:

Gratitude brings energy to life. When fatigue and despair pull you down, gratitude lifts your spirit. I help you focus on moments that energize you—a smile, laughter, rest, or a small accomplishment. Gratitude fuels vitality and reminds you that life's beauty is all around, waiting to be noticed.

Talk to Me:

"Archangel Samuel, help me find energy and hope through gratitude. Renew my spirit and show me life's simple, beautiful blessings. Thank you for your strength."

Archangel Zachariel

On Gratitude:

Gratitude is an act of strength. When life feels overwhelming, gratitude helps you stand firm, seeing gifts instead of problems. I guide you to appreciate how far you've come, even through adversity. From this grounded space of thankfulness, you can face any challenge with courage and resilience.

Talk to Me:

"Archangel Zachariel, help me stand strong in gratitude, even in difficult times. Show me the gifts in my journey and strengthen my spirit. Thank you for your guidance."

LIFE THROUGH ANGEL EYES

Archangel Jophiel

On Gratitude:

Gratitude makes life beautiful. I help you see splendor in the smallest details—a sunrise, a flower, a smile. Gratitude clears the mind of negativity, reminding you that life offers beauty at every turn. When you look through the lens of gratitude, even challenges become opportunities for growth.

Talk to Me:

"Archangel Jophiel, open my eyes to life's beauty and fill my heart with gratitude. Help me see blessings in every moment. Thank you for your light."

Archangel Laviah

On Gratitude:

Gratitude unlocks the wisdom of dreams. In the quiet moments between waking and sleeping, I show you the blessings you may have missed—opportunities, guidance, and inner truths. By practicing gratitude daily, you strengthen your intuition, aligning with the deeper flow of your life's path.

Talk to Me:

"Archangel Laviah, guide me to dream with gratitude and see the hidden blessings in my life. Help me connect to my deeper wisdom. Thank you for your insight."

Archangel Sandalphon

On Gratitude:

Gratitude grounds you in harmony. Music, nature, and movement carry frequencies of thankfulness that balance your energy and soothe your soul. I help you stay present, appreciating the world's rhythm and beauty. Gratitude connects heaven and earth, grounding your spirit while lifting your heart.

Talk to Me:

"Archangel Sandalphon, guide me to balance and harmony through gratitude. Let me stay present and grounded in the beauty of life. Thank you for your peace."

Archangel Jeremiel

On Gratitude:

Gratitude comes from reflection. I help you pause and review your life, seeing how moments of pain shaped you and joy sustained you. Gratitude doesn't ignore struggles but honors them as part of your growth. With this clarity, you move forward with grace, grounded in thankfulness.

Talk to Me:

"Archangel Jeremiel, guide me to reflect on my journey with gratitude. Help me find meaning in my experiences and embrace the blessings ahead. Thank you for your guidance."

Archangel Raguel

On Gratitude:

Gratitude restores balance in relationships. Misunderstandings or hurt often cloud what's good between people. I help you appreciate the efforts, kindness, and love of others, even in imperfect moments.

LIFE THROUGH ANGEL EYES

Gratitude dissolves tension, allowing relationships to heal and harmony to return.

Talk to Me:

"Archangel Raguel, help me see the good in my relationships and embrace gratitude for others. Bring harmony and appreciation into my life. Thank you for your support."

Archangel Haniel

On Gratitude:

Gratitude aligns you with grace. When you acknowledge life's cycles—times of growth, stillness, and change—you trust in divine timing. I help you find peace by appreciating where you are now. Gratitude creates balance, reminding you that each moment has purpose and beauty.

Talk to Me:

"Archangel Haniel, help me embrace life's flow with gratitude. Show me the grace in every moment and guide me to peace. Thank you for your light."

ANGEL WING WRAP-UP

Conclusion

As you close these pages, know this: you have not reached an end, but a beginning—a doorway to a deeper connection, not only with the angels but with yourself. These words were never meant to simply be read and put aside; they are threads meant to weave through your life, binding light to shadow, strength to vulnerability, and intention to action. The angels' guidance is not bound to these chapters—it moves with you, alive, ever-present, and waiting for you to notice.

This book is a map, but it does not give you the entire landscape at once. Instead, it reveals what you need, when you need it—a quiet voice in your moments of uncertainty, a hand steadying you when you falter, and a spark of clarity when the path is obscured. The angels have shown you how to navigate life's questions, pain, and revelations, gently nudging you back toward your soul's purpose. Their guidance does not vanish when you step away from these pages; it is already alive within you.

The intentions for using this book are as simple as they are profound: to remember you are never alone, to trust that wisdom surrounds you, and to recognize that even in silence, the angels are with you. When you find yourself wandering—feeling lost, unsure, or disconnected—return to these words. Each message carries an energy, a resonance, that will stir something within you, awakening forgotten strength, dormant dreams, and new possibilities.

The angels are your partners on this journey. They do not dictate, nor do they demand; they whisper, guide, and align you with the truth you already carry. To stay in touch with them, invite them in. Speak to them in your moments of joy, struggle, and stillness. Call on them,

LIFE THROUGH ANGEL EYES

in light and love, with words, thoughts, or even a simple breath of intention. Trust that they hear you—always.

Keep your heart open to their signs, for they speak through more than just words. They reveal themselves in the rhythms of nature, the lyrics of a song, the flicker of intuition, or the sudden sense of peace that feels like it came from nowhere. The more you listen, the clearer their presence will become.

As you move forward, know this: the angels are always near, woven into the fabric of your life, guiding you with love and light. They are here to help you remember who you are, to find your way, and to walk in alignment with your soul's purpose.

This is not goodbye; it is a promise. The angels' voices will remain with you, even in the quiet. All you need to do is listen, trust, and take that next step—knowing you are supported, surrounded, and deeply loved. Thank you, Angels.

www.ingramcontent.com/pod-product-compliance
Lightning Source LLC
Chambersburg PA
CBHW021142160426
43194CB00007B/659